The Girlfriend Trap reminded me of the standards we should set for those we allow in our lives. This book also challenged me to think critically about unhealthy dating practices. Read this book if you seek to be challenged and encouraged at the same time!

— **Stephanie Cassell, 25 years old**

The Girlfriend Trap asked questions that I didn't know to ask and gave me honest, unfiltered answers that I needed to hear. This book will arm young women with the knowledge they need to form the right kind of relationship. It's definitely a must-read.

— **Amiri Bradford, 17 years old**

The Girlfriend Trap is a book that challenges the current views on dating and relationships. Through her transparency and encouragement, Brittany forces young women to see themselves as they truly are...queens! Trust me when I say, these concepts are life-changing!

— **NaShara Neal, 24 years old**

This book is a great read! It opened my eyes to how much I am worth, and how I am worth the wait. It helped me understand what to do and what to not do when being pursued. Any single woman who has a desire to be married should read this book!

— **Brittany Okossi, 25 years old**

I initially thought there would be extreme viewpoints in this book and that some of the advice wouldn't be very practical. I definitely have a new perspective on dating. I see nothing wrong with simply courting a potential wife. I believe not having the boyfriend title helps me hold myself accountable and set clear intentions.

— **Jeffrey Knight, 27 years old**

This book really puts the steps of getting into a relationship into perspective, especially for a teen like myself. It taught me key points on how I should approach and maintain a relationship with someone on a deeper level. I would recommend this book to any young woman to help them better understand their self-worth and develop realistic expectations when entering a new relationship.

– Raina Ford, 15 years old

This book teaches women the importance of knowing their worth and the importance of building a relationship only on God's foundation.

– Ky Ellis, 24 years old

The Girlfriend Trap opened my eyes to so many things. I thought I knew a lot until I read this book. To be better is to do better and consistently growth in both knowledge and faith and this book provided a lot of that. It will change your life for the better. It will enlighten you in a way you never expected. You'll learn how much God loves you which will ultimately reveal your self-worth to yourself and those around you.

– Tiffany Keys, 29 years old

This book trumps all wishing and longing to be in a relationship due to loneliness. You are going to bypass a lot of fire with the knowledge that is in this book. Just amazing!

– Marcy Youngblood, 27 years old

The Girlfriend TRAP

The Bait, What the Trap Creates and Your Way of Escape

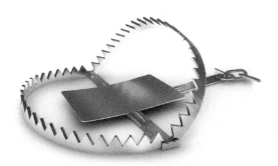

Brittany Marie Jones

She Abundantly Publishing, an imprint of She Abundantly LLC

Contents

Dedication

To my Father God in Heaven. Thank you for saving me and delivering me from the enemy. Thank you for giving me eternal life and showing me what real love and commitment looks like.

To my parents. Thank you for loving, caring and providing for me.

To my spiritual leaders. Thank you for seeing and nurturing what God put inside me.

To my mentors. Thank you for paving the way and leaving breadcrumbs for me to follow.

To the Davis Dynamic Duo. Thank you for encouraging, coaching and helping me be my greatest self. Thank you for being my on-demand strategist and book committee during the writing process.

To every guy that I have ever dated. Thank you for helping me realize my true worth. Because of you, now every girl who reads this will know their worth too. I thought about you on every page.

Preface

One day, I saw a boyfriend praise his girlfriend on social media and as he did that, he labeled her as his "helpmate." When I saw that, a fire set ablaze in my heart. This was not a fire that was set to keep people warm in the winter months or even provide heat to make those chocolatey gooey s'mores that melt in your mouth on a crisp fall evening. This was a consuming fire, the fire that someone sets ablaze to burn up something that is not supposed to be here.

This fire was the fire straight from heaven, set ablaze by God himself. The Bible refers to God as a Consuming Fire

"Therefore let us be grateful for receiving a kingdom that cannot be shaken, and thus let us offer to God acceptable worship, with reverence and awe, for our God is a consuming fire." – **Hebrews 12:28-29 (ESV)**

A helpmate is the righteous position that God created for a woman to be to a man in the context of love, commitment and purpose (Genesis 2:18), everything that a girlfriend is not. At that moment, as that boyfriend lifted up his girlfriend to God as "acceptable worship" for the whole world to see, I felt the impression of God say, "this is an unholy misrepresentation and perversion of my design for romantic love, and it must be burned up by fire."

Everything that I experienced and witnessed of what a girlfriend actually is came to a boiling overflow from my heart at that very moment and God told me it was time for me to share His heart with his daughters (and sons) concerning how he feels about this boyfriend-girlfriend culture.

God gave the message for this book to me in a matter of minutes but it took me 4 years to finally write and publish this. Insecurity, perfection, pressure and a whole lot of fear quickly sprang up within me as I began to write it all out because I knew this book was not going to be just a passion project or another goal that I could say I completed before moving on to the next one. I knew this book would be powerful, challenging and freeing all at the same time and I knew the enemy would not be happy with the truth that I am dropping for every woman to consume without limitations. I'm so glad I pushed through.

I wrote this book for the young woman who wishes someone would just see her and love her enough to snatch her out of the fire and give her clear direction when it comes to relationships. I wrote this book so that I could give to you what I did not receive as a girlfriend, the raw truth that sets you up for success in the future.

We live in a world and culture where people are afraid to step up and step out. Everyone seems to be okay with being a clone and following the norm. The norm is okay if that's what you are created to be, but you are not! If you are tired of following the crowd, then this book is for you. If you are a young woman who has settled for less but has always felt like you deserved more, this book is for you. I wrote this book for every young queen who has yet to realize her royal status. Don't be normal. Be royal.

PART 1

The Girlfriend Trap

CHAPTER 1

What Is a Girlfriend?

If you would have asked me this question as a teen, I probably would have given a surface answer or better yet, my answer would have been, "I don't know." All I knew was that I wanted to be one because that meant I would have a boy that I can call my own, a cute one at that. I would have a boy that would give me all the attention and affection that I desired, someone that I could physically touch, hold, and, well, let him do the same to me.

I became a girlfriend at the age of twelve, and it was a rude awakening of my heart, followed by years filled with multiple failed attempts at relationships. I had no clue what I was doing, and I could tell that he didn't either, nor the next guy, nor the guy after him. When you like a guy, the only thing that you know to do is to claim him as your own and do what you think boyfriends and girlfriends are supposed to do, hoping for the best. It's kind of like a game you play, except most of the time there are no winners in the end.

What is a girlfriend? I have asked myself this question over and over, and I can not come up with a **legit** answer. Even after being a girlfriend for a span of twelve years of my life, I got nothing. Why did I allow myself to be someone's girlfriend? What was it? What really were we doing?

Now, to the average person, if I asked them this question, I'm sure I would get responses like, "a girlfriend is someone that you really like. She is someone you spend time with and you can call your own. She is someone that will be there for you no matter what. She is a ride-or-die chick. You can talk to her about anything. You can hold her hand, kiss her, touch her body parts and have sex with her if you choose to. You can do whatever you want to do

3

with her." As a matter of fact, here are some responses I received when I asked this question.

A girlfriend is:

1. Your backbone, someone who is <u>supposed to</u> support you in <u>everything</u> you do.

2. A wifey in training.

3. Your best friend, homie and significant other *all in one*.

4. Someone <u>who's loyal</u> to you.

5. A girl who can be <u>your peace</u> when everything is going wrong. She is someone you can <u>confide and trust in</u>. You can learn from her and grow with her mentally, physically & spiritually.

6. A girl that loves you <u>no matter what</u> and is there to help you <u>with whatever</u> you need help with.

7. Someone who accepts you for you and is <u>always willing</u> to learn more about you. She <u>doesn't give up on you</u> or the relationship when things get rough.

8. A man's <u>happiness</u>.

9. Someone who's <u>always willing</u> to be a helping hand, not fully depending on the boyfriend to get things done for her, but independent enough to be able to hold her own.

10. Someone you can <u>move in with</u> and eventually get married to and have your <u>happily ever after</u> with.

Peep Game Queen: Notice the words I underlined. As we continue this girl chat I want you to hold on to those words as they will come up later and for good reason.

Okay, when you read this I'm sure you were agreeing with most, if not all of these definitions of a girlfriend. Yes, all this sounds good and looks really cute on an Instagram post, #RelationshipGoals. But when you think about it, how does being this "girlfriend" help you? With being your boyfriend's all in one, his peace and happiness, his place of confidence, you sticking by his side no matter what, helping him no matter what, loving him no matter what, never giving up on him and **giving him your everything** (because that's really what these definitions are describing here), how has this kind of life been for you? How is your heart? Is it whole and complete with no breakage? Do you feel your heart has been protected and cherished? Do you have confidence in the male gender and feel hopeful about your future with a man one day? Guy meets girl, they kiss and then ride off into the sunset. Your happily-ever-after dream right? If that's what we're expecting, we should really stick to movies.

What really happens in these boyfriend and girlfriend relationships? Let me summarize it for you: You give a guy your intimate conversation and time. You allow him into your private space and give him full access to everything you have, your heart and panties. You invest so much of yourself into him, even going so far as to moving in with him, having children with him and making all these committed-like decisions with him. Then... it ends! You give yourself in this way all because he has given you the title "girlfriend." For some reason, when you establish a guy as your boyfriend and you as his girlfriend, you subconsciously tell yourself that you are supposed to be the "most" to him and do the "most" with him, the absolute most. But *how many* guys need to fill this spot of boyfriend for you to realize that there is something flawed about this relationship system? If it's such a great position, then why is the turnover so high? Why does this position need to be filled every few months or years?

I was sitting down one day, and I began to think about all the relationships I have been in and the relationships I see around me. I thought about how they all started out so cute.

"Oooh, girl, he is so fine. He is really there for me. I think I love him already. I want to be with him and have all his babies."

You guys are always boo'd up. You take pictures together and post them, buy gifts for each other and go everywhere together. And then something happens that leads to a break-up, and you bingeing on break-up songs as you figure out who your next "ex" boyfriend will be. You move on so quickly, hoping to make the previous guy feel like he missed out on a good thing.

They say the best way to get over a guy is to get under a new one. But queen, doing that may temporarily make you feel better, but it doesn't heal you. Have you ever seen a wound heal by using a knife? Right! Turning to the same thing that hurt you to heal you (a guy) is counteractive even if the next guy seems like a better guy. A wound without proper knowledge and skill on how to heal it will only grow deeper and worse over time no matter how cute the social media pictures are.

I then began to think about all the damage that occurred during the relationship and after the break-up: the broken hearts, babies birthed into broken families, the anger, bitterness and unforgiveness. Not to mention the physical, emotional and spiritual baggage that we accumulate and carry with us for the rest of our lives. When Erykah Badu sang that song, "Bag lady," she was talking directly to you and I. At that moment, I sensed God ask me this question with so much clarity: "Could all this be because this kind of relationship was never supposed to exist?"

Wait, what? But how do you… what is he to me then if…..how does it work if you don't…? Crazy enough, I started to see His point and I knew the answer simply by how He asked the question. Yes! All this damage happens because this relationship system that we have accepted and adapted to was never God's intention when it comes to romance and the health of the human heart.

Check out these stats that I strongly believe are a result of how we date in today's culture.

"An estimated 55% of male and female teens have had sexual intercourse by age 18" **(CDC, 2017)**.

"Blacks (32%) are much less likely than whites (56%) to be married, and this gap has increased significantly over time. And black children (52%) are nearly three times as likely as white children (18%) and nearly twice as likely as Hispanic children (27%) to live with one parent" **(Pew Research, 2010)**.

"The U.S. has the world's highest rate of children living in single-parent households. Almost a quarter of U.S. children under the age of 18 live with one parent and no other adults (23%), more than three times the share of children around the world who do so (7%)" **(Pew Research, 2019)**.

"In 2018, unmarried women accounted for 85% of all abortions (mostly women age 20-29)" **(Abort73)**.

"The #1 reason for wanting to get an abortion was, 'not ready for a child'" **(Abort73).**

From that day forward, God and I continued to talk more about this dating culture, which is why you and I are having this girl talk right now. Let me just say this upfront: This girl chat does not come from bitterness, anger or hatred. In fact, I am quite healed and content. I am not a "used to be" girlfriend turned mad who wants to bash all girlfriend-boyfriend relationships because I had a bad experience. No! I wrote this book from an authentic place of love and genuine care for young women like you. I wrote this book because I began to really examine the dating life, not only mine but also the people closest to me and far away. I have studied culture, the generation before, the generation now and the generation coming up; all of which have practiced this way of dating, and I think I speak for most women when I say something is off.

May I ask you a few questions? Did you grow up in a single-parent household? Do you have daddy and/or mommy wounds from an absent father and a bitter mother who just couldn't seem to heal from her man-hurt? Do you feel like you suffer(ed) from it?

Most of us can answer yes to all of these questions and why do you think that is? Could it be because our parents dated the same way that theirs did too? Many of our grandparents may have gotten married but most of the time, the marriage itself was something you didn't want to model after. Getting married because you got pregnant or marrying a serial cheater and sticking it out in the name of fear is less than ideal. Let me say this, the journey during any relationship can be determined by how you start it. What you use to build the foundation of the relationship will oftentimes be what you use to keep the relationship standing. And for most, that foundation is layered with bricks of ignorance, low self-esteem and no guidance from God above.

>  #TheGirlfriendTrap
>
> *Boyfriends and girlfriends are man-made, not God-made. You can tell by all the damage they cause and the countless refunds being requested.*
>
> #TheGirlfriendTrap

The truth is God never intended for His daughters to endure so much damage and pain when it comes to romantic relationships; guy after guy, year after year and generation after generation. He desires us to know the truth about our dating culture and here it is: Boyfriends and girlfriends are man-made, not God-made. You can tell by all the damage they cause and the countless refunds being requested.

Why Girls Become Girlfriends

Here are some reasons why girls often become **girlfriends:**

- She is bored. She has nothing else going on in her life so she finds her high in another person.
- She is looking for male love and affection to make up for an absent father.
- She is insecure about herself and feels a guy will give her worth and validation.
- To get experience. (I had a girl tell me this and, until this day, I am still confused as to what experience she is looking for.)
- She has a fear of missing out.
- Peer pressure.
- She wants to go out on dates and possibly get free stuff.
- She believes that's what she is supposed to do.
- She wants a guy to claim and protect her because she never had a man do that for her...the daddyless-heart syndrome.

Do you find yourself on this list? To be honest, every last one of those was my reason for becoming a girlfriend and so young at that. But pay close attention. There is one ingredient that they all have in common: *emptiness*! And can I tell you something that I learned the hard way? When you act and behave from a place of emptiness instead of fullness, the end result will be empty as well, if not more empty than when you started.

As we continue with what I believe will be one of the best conversations you and I will ever have, I want to ask you a question and, hopefully, challenge your thinking in the process.

What does a guy have to be or do for you to be his *girlfriend*? Circle your answer(s)

1. Be good looking
2. Show you attention
3. Be popular or famous
4. Say he loves you
5. Nothing
6. Have faith in God
7. Have a car
8. Pay your bills or buy you gifts (have money)
9. Be respectful and kind
10. Have great intelligence
11. Have sex with you
12. Be the father of your child

If you circled any one of these answers on this list, let me challenge you and possibly offend you, (disrupt your normal way of thinking) when I say that reality is, it doesn't take much for a guy to have you as his *girlfriend*. Now, if this is shocking to you, don't worry! I'm about to explain why in the next few chapters. I'm the first to admit that I circled most of those answers, especially the "have faith in God" one, and realized that it still didn't take much for a guy to have me as his *girlfriend*.

My desire is that, by the time you finish reading this book, your eyes open to see just how valuable you are and that your criteria for allowing a guy to have you as his own narrows down to the most important one. I will be spelling out for you why you must have standards when it comes to being a woman in this world. Also, trust me when I say that raising your standards when it comes to dating is for your own benefit and protection. The decisions you make today will always affect your tomorrows and your kid's tomorrows, even those yet to be born.

Here we go queen! Let's crack open the skull and take a look into the mind of a girlfriend. Are you ready? Of course, you are.

CHAPTER 2
The Girlfriend Mindset

That's just it. Being a girlfriend is a mentality that you have. It's an attitude or setting of the mind. It's how you think and feel about yourself and it's a thinking that falls short of the mentality that you are to have as a young woman who was created by a committed and romantic God.

Think about your daughter(s) or future daughters. Based on your current understanding and mentality as a girlfriend, are you excited for her to one day get out into the dating world and find true love or do you tense up with fear by just the thought of her possibly experiencing anything you've experienced when it comes to guys? If it's the latter, that's a tell-tale sign that the way you have viewed yourself and interacted with guys has been nothing worth repeating.

We have heard it said before: Every young woman goes through a few heartbreaks before she finds "the one," and we have accepted this broken saying as truth. Why? Because it has been a reality for so many of us. Unfortunately, it will continue to be if you keep the same mindset that you have now. It will be more like *settling* for "the one" because you got tired of starting all over again.

Does it have to be this way? **Why do so many women experience so much heartbreak as a girlfriend?** Here is one reason, because she thinks that being a girlfriend is her mountain top. She thinks that it's the end all be all position for her, and if that's the case, then she has to give it ALL she has to keep the role.

She believes that in order to get and keep a guy she has to be everything to him in hopes of him choosing her to be his forever. It's attached to a poverty mindset. I don't have and I don't know how to get it so I will grab a hold and hold on to whatever is available now, "no matter what." She thinks that being a girlfriend is equal to being a wife, and it shows by her willingness to be so open and available to every guy who gives her that title. Remember those words that I underlined in the previous chapter? Queen, let's look at those words again.

Here are keywords in the "role" of a girlfriend:

1.   Supposed to
2.   Everything (meaning ALL things)
3.   Loyal
4.   (His) peace
5.   Confide and trust in
6.   No matter what
7.   With whatever
8.   Doesn't give up
9.   Happiness
10.   Always willing
11.   Move in with
12.   Happily ever after

When I asked these young women what their definition of a girlfriend was, for the most part, I saw nothing wrong with what they said in the actual words in and of themselves. They were essentially saying how they desire to be in a committed relationship and to be able to give themselves to a man in ways that no other woman can or should. Those are healthy aspirations.

Desiring to be in a romantic relationship with a man is in our DNA, so to speak. We are wired to *attract*, mate and procreate. But this is where we fall off the cliff; we have these beautiful and healthy desires, but we don't have any instruction or direction to go with them.

Why do I say that? Well, what is one word that all those words and phrases that I underlined have in common? (Whatever you think of, go ahead, say it out loud to yourself). I can tell you what comes to my mind: commitment.

It sounds to me that a girlfriend is supposed to be more than an actual girl that's a friend. Just reading the role of a girlfriend shows me that the average young woman is giving her boyfriend things that only a wife should give. That's why most of the time the relationship ends up not working out. Somewhere along the way the roles of wife and girlfriend get mixed up in translation and she tries to operate under a legal system of commitment as a wife but has no legal right to do so as a girlfriend.

It's like arriving at the oval office but trying to use your high school badge to unlock the door, (and just for the record, I am not referring to the guy as the oval office but I am referring to the system of commitment as the oval office).

According to the Oxford English Dictionary, a role is "the function assumed or part played by a person or thing in a particular situation." Those words I highlighted show the "role" that the average young woman assumes she is supposed to fulfill as a girlfriend to her boyfriend.

But my question is where did the description of this role come from and who determined her function? Can one trace it in the books? Maybe! But I can tell you one thing for sure; this script was planted in broad daylight in hopes that you would read it and audition. It's a strategic plan to dethrone you from your queendom status as a "one and only" committed woman, only to be tossed to the bottom of the barrel, fighting and competing with other women, giving all you got just to be a "one of many" thespian (turned lesbian). Girrrrrl Listen!

Speaking of thespian (which is an actress), this role of being a girlfriend is not something you just jump into. You have to study it. You have to perfect your craft so that you can deliver and portray the true intention and passion that the writer wanted a girlfriend to have.

This is why girls begin their training at such a young age. Take me for example. I started training in kindergarten as I tried to call this boy I liked my boyfriend. I would be all touchy-feely with him and oftentimes would try to snuggle up with him when no one was looking.

See, it takes years to get this role down packed and once you get into the role, you never get out! You become a type cast, which is an actress that's repeatedly assigned to the same type of role. Why? Because she is so dang good at it. And by she I mean you.

You have become such a success at being a girlfriend that it becomes the only role available to you. You are so good at being everything to a guy that you play this role again and again and...again and... again. Whether it be to multiple guys, or to one guy for multiple sequels, a girlfriend has become your lifelong assignment. Coincidence? I think not.

Daddy Wounds Produce Perfect Girlfriends

This leads me to the **second reason why girls experience so much heartbreak as a girlfriend**; she wants the role so badly that she will try to get it at any cost, even to the point of going out into the dating world uncovered. Every young woman is to be covered by a male authority who is called to protect her and that male is her father. A natural father is a beautiful and tangible representation of the heavenly father, and he is called to provide protection, wisdom, guidance, love and much more to his children.

As we continue this conversation about fathers, I want you to know that even if you don't have a healthy father figure in sight, you always have the healthiest and perfect covering from your heavenly father. He fixes all things that your natural father may have broken if you allow Him to.

A father is a young woman's protective covering who has healthy authority in her life. That authority includes making rules or decisions, giving orders and enforcing obedience to those rules and orders. He keeps bad things out while preserving and helping to mature the good things within her. He teaches her to live in order so that she can stay on a path of safety. That safety preserves her heart as she goes through this jungle called life...and men!

I want to share with you what I have learned as a girlfriend, what I have observed in other girlfriends and what God has revealed to me about this role through my mentor and wise counsel.

The mentality of a girlfriend is one of disorder. What that means is this mentality does not follow order or direction. She wanders off the path of safety from underneath her protective covering or in many cases, never allowing herself to be protected at all. She does this to go and audition for a guy that has no right or permission to have her as his girl, nor does he have any responsibility to protect her like her father does. That means he won't care to protect her heart and be integral towards her in every way possible. Almost all of the time she will get hurt and broken in some kind of way because of that.

What is order? Order, simply put, means to arrange in a row. I like to think of it this way: It is an established process or a way of doing something to achieve a proper outcome.

Safety and the blessings of God are only found within order, not outside it. That means when you follow order, God will open doors for you to walk through so that you may advance in life. The Word of God is established order, and anything we do outside of it is disorder. Take this example to help: To get to step five, you must first go through step 1, 2, 3 and 4. Each step brings about a level of security, confidence and assurance. Because you traveled from step 1 to 2, you can expect step 3 to be there and be sure that step 4 is there to follow. With each step, you obtain everything you need inorder to go to the next one. Without order, a process goes wrong and becomes very chaotic, creating disorder.

Disorder means to destroy the order of or throw something or someone into confusion to where things become fused together and indistinguishable. This means you will be lost with no understanding of what step to take next in a particular area. Wow! Does this sound familiar in your dating life? That confusion is meant to disrupt the peace or unity between the one giving the orders and the one receiving them. This ultimately throws you off the path of safety because you are no longer in tune with the one keeping you safe, like your father.

I can totally relate to the process of order. As a clinical laboratory scientist in the health profession, I have learned that order is everything and one wrong move or short cutting my way through the steps to any procedure can cost a patient their entire life.

The same goes for your life as a young woman, especially your dating life. Your process involves learning how to hear and be led by the voice of a good father, or the one who creates order for your protection. And as he does life with you, his wisdom will guide you as **a daughter** who is maturing into **womanhood,** learning to be **a wife** who will one day be ready to stand alongside another man of order in holy **matrimony.** Queen, did you catch that order? If not, check out the process below.

Daughter → Woman → Wife (in mentality) → Wife (in reality)

Step 1   **Step 2**   **Step 3**   **Step 4**

Step 1: Daughter – needs to be raised and taken care of by father/family

Step 2: Woman – when sexual maturity meets mental, emotional and spiritual maturity

Step 3: Wife (in mentality) – has a helpful mindset, mission-minded and ready to begin her God-given assignment with a man

Step 4: Wife (in reality) – you can now give birth and reproduce the same kind as you and raise them up to follow order and worship God

Note: these steps are not mutually exclusive, meaning one excludes the other. These steps are mutually inclusive, meaning one includes the other.

If this angers you or makes you feel a certain way to know that you as a young woman desperately need a healthy father's direction, love and protection in your life, I can tell you right now that how you may be thinking or feeling is nothing but a trauma response. Trauma is a distressing experience that happens to you that your mind or emotions can't process at that time. This results in wounding to your being either mentally, emotionally or physically, depending on what the traumatic event was. The more personal the traumatic event, the deeper the wound and hurt in that individual. A parent missing in a child's life is traumatic to that child and it stunts their development, which almost always will show up in that person's life through their perverted or misuse of things. They will misuse and abuse relationships, their body and substances like drugs, food and alcohol. Most women in our day and age are wounded from the trauma of an absent father or the presence of a bad or immature one. Either way, it has caused you to build up a wall or a false sense of security that has you believing that you don't need a man for anything and that you can strictly depend on yourself (or women) to be successful in life.

It is true, you can move forward and achieve great things in life but just because you can do something on the outside does not mean it's the best way to do it and that you are healthy on the inside. Your bad choices in guys, failed relationships, decisions made from low self-esteem and the deep trust issues you have with men, that even bring out tears to this day, are all proof that shows you that your heart needs both a mother and a father.

Your heart was designed not only to be nurtured by a mother and shown how to be a woman by that same mother, but it was also made to be loved and cared for by a father. A father has the God-given authority to call out and establish true identity in you and teach you how to be treated by a man.

No matter how great women are, they are not men and never will be. They can never come from a man's point of view, and God did not create a woman to be without a healthy and mature male presence in her life. If this has been your reality, it has been so because circumstances have made it this way and not because you chose it to be this way. Only a woman who has never had a healthy father's direction, love and protection in her life will turn her nose up and roll her eyes at the idea of submitting to a father's guidance in this way.

*"Hear, O children, the instruction of a father, And pay attention [and be willing to learn] so that you may gain understanding and intelligent discernment. For I give you good doctrine; Do not turn away from my instruction. When I was a son with my father (David), Tender and the only son in the sight of my mother (Bathsheba), He taught me and said to me, 'Let your heart hold fast my words; Keep my commandments and live. Get [skillful and godly] wisdom! Acquire understanding [actively seek spiritual discernment, mature comprehension, and logical interpretation]! Do not forget nor turn away from the words of my mouth.'" – **Proverbs 4:1-5 (AMP)**

As a young woman who has lived the majority of her life without a healthy father figure, which led to complete disorder, I have now come to greatly value order, and the ones who have created it for me...God and my brother-in-law. Being able to follow sound guidance and allowing structure into your life saves you in more ways than one. If your heart is open, by the time we are done with this girl chat, you will be on your own path to safety and God's blessings. Order in your life helps you dodge people who hate order, and those are the kind of guys who will break your heart and destroy your life.

Speaking of guys, let's talk more about them.

CHAPTER 3

The Uncovering

Every man has been given a God-ordained, healthy level of authority so that he can produce order on the earth. This authority is something that he doesn't just start operating in from the day he is born. He has to grow up and mature in it. It's up to him to learn the voice of God so that he may use his authority in a way that *makes God known*. A man who is mature in his authority will always honor and respect the authority of another man.

When it comes to wanting to pursue you romantically, that mature man will go to the one you belong to, to be screened (so to speak) and for permission to go after you. Who do you belong to? Your father! And by father, I mean your natural father (if he is fit to lead in your life) and/or your heavenly father (who should always be addressed as the covering over your life).

Hear me, queen. In no way am I denying the wisdom of women. You need a whole squad of wisdom surrounding you to help you along this dating process (we will talk more about that later) but what I am saying is you need that covering whether it be a natural father figure or not. This is good because fathers are there to protect and preserve your heart. Never forget that. Fathers can see things in other men that women may overlook. Don't believe me? Ask a wise man who can tell you about the discernment he has when it comes to another guy. Go to www.sheabundantly.com/FathersProtection to listen to one right now.

Fathers are there to make sure you are being pursued by a protector and not a predator who just wants to "try you out" and discard you when he is done with you (like what your average boyfriend does today).

Fathers are there to make sure that this guy does not turn you into anything less than what you're created to be. That means he makes sure that you are promoted as a young woman and not demoted.

You are under your father's authority and until another man shows himself worthy to cover you as a husband, he has no authoritative voice in your life, and it's wise that you do not give him one. A girlfriend gives a boyfriend an authoritative voice in her life when there is no legal ground for him to have one. This means she allows him to come into her life and lead her in thoughts, decisions and through sex, which often leads to her and his destruction in many ways. That's the issue. When a young woman has not had a healthy father figure to cover and guide her, she is more prone to allowing a bootleg guy to take that spot of authority, and most of the time, he's immature himself and not ready to lead her.

 #TheGirlfriendTrap

You are under your father's authority and until another man shows himself worthy to cover you as a husband, he has no authoritative voice in your life, and it's wise that you do not give him one.

#TheGirlfriendTrap

What happens when you take shortcuts through any process of order? You break that order into pieces. When a guy does not go to your father to be approved to pursue you AND have you for his own, and instead, you go to him and submit to his authority (or his voice) behind your father's back, that is high-level disorder. If that's not clear, then let me say it this way; the guy approaches you, gets all up in your head, tells you what you want to hear and wins your heart over so that he can now claim you as his girl (and you are not married to him which means you are really not his girl)...DISORDER!

Do you see the issue with that? He dishonored your covering in a quest to be your covering. But did you peep game? To make a grab at anything or anyone that does not belong to you is illegal behavior. It's called stealing and most guys do this under the title "boyfriend."

Just so you won't think I'm trying to paint a false picture here, how many guys do you know even acknowledge a young woman's covering (either her natural father or Father God) first before claiming her as his girl? Close to zero.

How many girls do you know, including yourself, willingly become a guy's girlfriend with no guidance from her father (either her natural father or Father God), really with no guidance at all for that matter? Right! Almost every girl you know! It is our cultural norm but just because it's normal does not mean it's healthy or godly.

Every woman is to be covered by a legal male authority from the day she is born until the day she dies. The path of a woman who desires marriage goes from being a daughter covered by her father to being a wife covered by her husband. So, where does a girlfriend fit in? She doesn't! A girlfriend is not an in-between phase from daughter to wife no matter how much we try to fit her in. She is not a wifey in training. A girlfriend was never a role you were called to assume because there is no covering for her.

She is an uncovered woman that has willingly and illegally submitted herself to the authority of an immature man. She assumes the role of an illegitimate woman, and where there is no legitimacy there is no law and order!

This may offend you as you are reading this because you may have become married to this girlfriend role but the truth is, whether you want to admit it or not, that guy is a thief and you are now stolen goods. He has taken you for himself:

> #TheGirlfriendTrap
>
> *A girlfriend was never a role you were called to assume because there is no covering for her.*
>
> #TheGirlfriendTrap

"You are *my girl* and no one else's," without actually "paying a price," if you will, or sacrificing something of great value to have you. And you let him do it.

The reason why there is so much confusion around the role of a girlfriend is because there is no honorable function for her, and there is no law and order for her to follow. This is why you see girlfriends doing what wives do. Since she has no legit function of her own, she has to steal the script from the one who does. He's stealing, you're stealing, it's one big heist!

When a guy does not submit to order, he dishonors your father as well as yourself. We call this kind of guy a wild animal. Wild animals are those who live in the "wilderness" or live a wild life. They do not follow order or a voice of authority, but instead, are led by their bodily instincts.

They go after what they see and if it looks good, good enough to eat, then the hunt is on. This is why I encourage young women to submit to a father figure whether it be a blood father, a trusted male authoritative figure, and always God the father! She has to stay protected for one, but she also must give the guy who is interested in her another authoritative figure to submit to and be held accountable to concerning her.

But if you as a young woman willingly give yourself to a wild animal, it's because you have wandered off from that covering into the wilderness for him to even have access to you. Wild animals only mate with other wild animals which means that neither one of you follows order or honors the authority of your father. Yes, queen, that means you are wild in nature too. And just like scripture says, the only path that's available for irrational thinkers like wild animals is one of being caught in a trap and destroyed.

"But these, like irrational animals, creatures of instinct, born to be caught and destroyed, blaspheming about matters of which they are ignorant, will also be destroyed in their destruction" – **2 Peter 2:12 (ESV)**

How Girls Become Girlfriends

Let me show you how young women actually become girlfriends. Remember when I said that every man has been given a level of authority? It comes from this Scripture.

"Now the Lord God had formed out of the ground all the wild animals and all the birds in the sky. He brought them to the man to see what he would name them; *and whatever the man called each living creature, that was its name.* So the man gave names to all the livestock, the birds in the sky and all the wild animals." – **Genesis 2:19-20 (NIV)**

God gave the man the authority to name ALL living creatures. This included wild animals which means it takes a godly man to properly bring out one's identity, even in those who are wild in nature. But it didn't stop with animals. Check this out:

"Adam *named his wife* Eve, because she would become the mother of all the living." – **Genesis 3:20 (NIV)**

Wow! Not only was he given the authority to name animals, but he was also given the authority to name humans. Yes! Women may birth humans, but it's up to man to name them and to establish order and identity for the family. Think about it. A man named you and you will always carry the name of a male authoritative figure. It's your last name.

A name equates to authority, but not only that; it also equates to an assignment. If you didn't notice, most people live out their name. After the man named her Eve, what was her assignment? Let's read it again.

"Adam named his wife Eve, because *she would become the mother of all the living.*" – **Gen 3:20 (NIV)**

Do you see that? The man named her according to what she would do. Eve surely became the mother of the world, and it was the man that brought that out of her. And let me tell you something, that's a beautiful thing. Any man who hears the voice of God will only assign to you what your father (in this case, God) says you are and what he created you to do, nothing less.

Now, don't get it twisted. God created you and has given you your roles, functions and assignments before any man has a chance to establish them here on earth. Check this out.

"Then the Lord God said, 'It is not good that the man should be alone; I will make him *a helper* fit for him.'" – **Genesis 2:18 (NIV)**

Before the man ever knew her, could cover her (have authority over her), name her (Eve), assign her a role (as a wife) and give her an assignment (become the mother of all the living), her father, God, already gave her a role, function and assignment. He gave her the role of helper, which is essentially what a wife is, and a GREAT role I might add. He gave her the function to assist or help the man and the assignment to fulfill the mission God gave them. What was she supposed to help the man do? Check it out.

"So God created man in his own image, in the image of God he created him; male and female he created them. And God blessed them. And God said to them, '*Be fruitful* and *multiply* and *fill the earth* and *subdue it*, and *have dominion over* the fish of the sea and over the birds of the heavens and over every living thing that moves on the earth.'" – **Genesis 1:27-28 (NIV)**

The woman was equally told along with the man to:

1. **Be fruitful**= produce good things over and over again.

2. **Multiply and fill the earth** = fill the earth with people and God's goodness.
3. **Subdue it** = bring the world under your control.
4. **Have dominion over it** = completely rule over it and establish the highest order. That means to cause the earth and everything in it to obey God's law.

Wow! How amazing is that? Her "becoming the mother of all the living" was fulfilling the assignment to be fruitful, multiply and fill the earth, subdue it and have dominion over it.

But did you catch it, queen? It is up to the man to help establish that order here on earth. Why? Because God is a God of order, and He will always have the authoritative male figure in your life to bear the weight and responsibility concerning you. For example, God can't make you a legal wife without an authoritative man present to do it, and in this case, that authoritative man will be your husband.

If that man is mature, then there will never be a misassignment of you. I want you to see the connection here. Every man, and I mean EVERY MAN, has the authority to name a woman and assign her a role whether it be legally or illegally. This particular man in this Scripture, Genesis 3:20, was operating in his God-given authority, and he named the woman whom he legally had authority over because he was her husband. That means he had permission from her father (God) to cover, name and assign her a role which gave her an assignment.

But what happens when a man who has no legal authority to cover and name you (because he's not married to you) assigns you a role? Right, he assigns you the wrong role. When a man has no legal authority to cover and name you, he assigns you the wrong role.

You take on a role that was never assigned to you. This places you out of order, out of safety, out of God's blessing and ultimately causing you to function illegitimately in a role that was not authorized by God. And that role is that of girlfriend. Hear me, queen, a girlfriend is not just a title, it's a mentality and an illegitimate role that you function in.

The Assignment of a Girlfriend

What that means is you agree to the mission of a girlfriend and you take on the *assignment* of a girlfriend. What is the mission and assignment of a girlfriend? Here it is: **A girlfriend's mission is to NOT help a man but to break a man down, and her assignment is to only be a man's source of sexual pleasure and to produce illegitimate children for him.** That's it!! Instead of you being the mother of LIFE, you become the producer of death. You become the carrier and producer of brokenness, spiritually, emotionally and physically.

> 66 #TheGirlfriendTrap
>
> **A girlfriend's assignment is to be a man's source of sexual pleasure and to produce children for him.**
>
> #TheGirlfriendTrap 99

I have seen this play out in my life (minus the kids) and in the lives of so many women far too many times. It ALL makes sense. Think about it. Why do you think boyfriend and girlfriend relationships are always full of pain and chaos? Why do you think they always end, and end in an unhealthy way? Why do you think it's so hard, extremely hard, for boyfriends and girlfriends to NOT have sex even though God specifically and graciously reserves sex for a husband and wife only? It's because girlfriends and boyfriends are designed in disorder and to produce more disorder and brokenness. Boyfriends and girlfriends are designed to have sex (against God's law and order) and most end up doing it, falling victim to this trap.

Peep Game Queen: If you want to honor God with your body and reserve sex for marriage, you will struggle big time as a girlfriend. I will tell you how to not struggle with that later during our chat. Keep reading.

Take a hard look at all the girlfriends in the world, even your own life. What are these women doing with these guys? Participating in emotionally unhealthy ways with these guys, having sex with them and producing multiple kids for them. Queen, point out the lie. I don't believe you can! This is why "baby momma" is now a title that women have accepted because that is essentially her role, to have sex and produce children for a man. It's just an extension of a girlfriend

Most women I know who are girlfriends or who had been girlfriends, had sex with the guy and/or become his baby momma, whether she aborted the child or not. I have had teenagers, grown women, Christian women, women who don't know God, all confide in me and prove this to be true. A girlfriend can't get away from it. Because once you say yes to being a girlfriend, the forces that created this role will break you down and make sure that you perform your duties no matter how much you try to resist. It's just a matter of time.

 #TheGirlfriendTrap

Once you say yes to being a girlfriend, the forces that created this role will break you down and make sure that you perform your duties no matter how much you try to resist. It's just a matter of time.

#TheGirlfriendTrap

Queen, I want you to understand that the reason why this happens, no matter how hard you try to avoid it, is because this system of dating has been in place way before any of us came to this earth. It's a system that is established and will not change. You may have heard it before; it's called concubinage. Uh oh, it just got real!

CHAPTER 4
Concubinage

I would like to thank my mentor, Tiffany Buckner, for introducing me to this message of concubinage. What you are about to read is a combination of wisdom from her, the Holy Spirit and my own research concerning this topic. Let's go!

Concubinage is a system of old that can be found sprinkled into human civilization throughout history between men and women and it is still alive today. A concubine was a woman that a man acquired for himself that had a lesser status than a wife. Does this not sound familiar already? It should!

According to The New World Encyclopedia, "The concubine relationship is based on the power that one person has over another, typically a man's power over a woman." And in some cultures today, women concubines are viewed as objects that the man acquires to show off his high status or rank, and the more women he has, the more important or valuable the man seems to be in his society.

This is why men in our culture, and really all around the world, are often praised for having multiple women while women are condemned for having multiple men. It is because the man is believed to have more power over the woman than the woman over the man. As we have already discussed, there is some truth to that statement, but it's not true that men are to take that power and misuse, abuse, oppress and hoard women as they do today.

This power and authority was given to a man so that he may use it to create order and beauty on the earth, making a woman a wife, not a toy, as both, with equal essence as God image-bearers, honor and worship God. Think of God's intention of this power and authority as like a foundation that a beautiful home is supposed to be built on: stable, supportive, unbreakable and capable of holding the weight placed on it. It is the piece that the home is built on so that it can provide shelter and protection from life's storms.

Instead, men have inverted and perverted that foundation, like an upside-down home, and anything heavy that is wrongly placed above the head will only come crashing down, destroying anyone or anything underneath it. This misuse of power and authority is what created concubines in the first place.

The word concubine literally means to lie down with. That means when a woman lied down (had sex) with a man she was not married to, she became his concubine, a woman that he had acquired for himself but had a lesser status than a wife.

She would often be labeled as a "second class" wife which still made her lower status no better. This type of behavior is talked about a lot in the Old Testament of the Bible because this was an accepted way of doing relationships when it came to men and women in that culture. It does not mean it was right or that it was God's intention for relationships; it just means it was accepted as a cultural norm, and let me tell you this, it is STILL accepted today! We just call it by a different name, girlfriend.

Concubines were oftentimes women who were maid-servants or slaves, captives from war or even free women. Her main role was to provide children for a man to increase his household which included his name and wealth, and to be his source of sexual pleasure.

Many times, when a wife was barren or could not bear children, she would hand over her female maid-servant to her husband to bear him children (particularly sons) so that the name of the man could be carried on, on the earth. Most women who took on this role were in some type of bondage whether it be legally or in the mind. Some women were even sold to men by their father to be that man's concubine as a payment of a debt that the father owed.

Still, there were other women who were free and willingly sold themselves to be a man's concubine out of desperation because she would otherwise be homeless or have to resort to prostitution to make a living. She was unprotected and susceptible to all sorts of horrible crimes. Why? **Because she had no male covering.**

Although, there were laws in place to protect the role of a concubine; for example, the man had to provide food and shelter for her etc., the concubine still did not have the rights of a wife and oftentimes, when the wife had a child, her children would receive the inheritance from the father over the children of the concubine. Consider the example of Abraham, his wife Sarah, and their son Issac vs. Abraham, his concubine Hagar and their son Ishmael in the Bible.

"And Abraham said to God, 'Oh that Ishmael might live before you!' God said, 'No, but Sarah your wife shall bear you a son, and you shall call his name Isaac. I will establish my covenant with him as an everlasting covenant for his offspring after him.'" – **Genesis 17:18-19 (ESV)**

Once a woman had sex with a man, she became his property. He would call her "his girl" in today's terms. And when she became his girl (or one of his women), she often stayed his girl (or one of his women) with a status lesser than his wife. She never went out and became a wife on her own by way of another man because she already belonged to the man who concubined her. WOW! That means he could summon her to have sex with him anytime he wanted to and she went.

Girlfriends today are the same way. Have you ever noticed that once you have sex with a guy, he looks at you differently, becomes possessive of you, and it becomes hard for you to walk away from him physically and emotionally? I have. I've lived long enough to watch this dynamic play out in the lives of many, including my own.

Guys that I had sex with in my teen and young adult years continued to occupy a space in my soul after they were gone, and at some point, they all reached back out to me looking to see how I was doing. The crazy thing about that is, it was always years past my last interaction with them.

Flattering? Girl, please! It's because they were trying to eat again from where they once ate before. Because they had sex with me, they viewed me as their property and were trying to summon me to their bedroom again to have sex with me, only to put me away until they wanted to use me again for their sexual pleasure. I was concubined and didn't even know it.

Peep Game Queen: The next time an ex. reaches out to you, just know it's not because he loved you and misses you. It's because he views you as his own personal booty on demand. Concubinage is truly at work here. BLOCK HIM!

You Gave Him Power to Play You

Why does this happen like this? Queen, let me share something with you that school has never taught you, and that you won't learn in mainstream media: Once you have sex with a guy, you legally give him power and authority over you! This is a spiritual law, and spiritual law always trumps the law of this land.

> #TheGirlfriendTrap
>
> *Once you have sex with a guy, you legally give him power and authority over you!*
>
> #TheGirlfriendTrap

Sex is God's creation and it is regulated by God's law (His Word). Once you have sex with a person, God's spiritual law, the consequences that come from it whether it be blessings or curses, will ALWAYS come into play in your life no matter what. It does not matter what you believe, what that song on the radio says, what pornography says or what your family and friends have told you about sex. You are not above God's law and truth be told, there are many women, young and old, who are living oppressed lives because they are under the power of a guy, or guys, whom they are not supposed to be under. That's heavy!

Consider this: In God's eyes, the moment you have sex with a guy, it signifies that a marriage has happened between you two. No, really! That is the true ceremony of marriage, and it still is to this day because God's design for sex never changes and it never will.

Let me show you that I'm speaking facts.

"Therefore a man shall leave his father and his mother and hold fast to his wife, and they shall become one flesh." – **Genesis 2:24 (ESV)**

"Do you not know that your bodies are members of Christ? Shall I then take the members of Christ and make them members of a prostitute? Never! Or do you not know that he who is joined to a prostitute becomes one body with her? For, as it is written, 'The two will become one flesh.'" – **1 Corinthians 6:15-16 (ESV)**

In both Scriptures, **hold fast** and **joined** are the same kind of action which is a permanent gluing together and they both result in "the two becoming one." The two becoming one represents marriage in the Bible. What these Scriptures, specifically 1 Corinthians 6:16, are implying is that the way the two become one is through the act of sex.

When a man has sex with you, the authority that was given to him by God is now put to work whether legally or illegally and by that authority, he has to give you a role and an assignment. In a legal marriage, that role is a wife. The thing is, when that sexual act is not legal, when it's done outside God's law concerning sex, which is sex void of truth and integrity, when he has not honored this present world law as law now has us to go through a marriage process to make marriage legal here on earth, when he did not go to God for permission to have you in the first place, **he has defiled the relationship and has misused and abused his authority**.

And by that abuse, he has given you a role that is less than a wife, similar to that of a concubine. If he can't legally assign you the role of his wife, by spiritual law, he has to assign you something lesser, and it will always be something that is beneath God's desire and purpose for you.

The assignment of a wife, in summary, is to be an aid and helper to her husband, to submit to him as he submits to God so that the mission God has given that union be completed with grace and excellence. But get this, any assignment less than that of a wife will still be fulfilled because the woman has still submitted to that man's authority that he used illegally. Yes, the man may have abused his authority but she allowed it, YOU allowed it, and if girlfriend is the role that she accepted, then the assignment of a girlfriend she will fulfill...sex and babies, sex and babies.

We identified that a concubine is similar to the modern-day girlfriend, but I also want to point out that there are subroles to her that carry the same illegitimate status as she and is equally as perverted if not more perverted than a girlfriend.

The role that you allow a guy to assign to you is all dependent on how you have allowed that guy to interact with you. Let's break it down: You are his girlfriend if he is not married, his side chick if he is married, or his babymomma if you bore his child. In some instances, you are his ALL IN ONE. He stamps you by how he interacts with you, but none-the-less, they are all illegitimate roles.

I wanted to spell that out to show you why there is so much damage and delay in the life of a young woman as she goes from daughter to wife, that's if she ever makes it to wife at all. She takes on *one too many* illegitimate roles that she should have never said yes to. In fact, most daughters never make it to being a wife because she accepts the role of girlfriend (along with her subroles) and builds her whole life there, and get this, even if she actually gets married.

Did you know that you can be married and still be a girlfriend? How? A girlfriend is a mindset that you have to kill. So, even if you get married, the girlfriend in you will fight to live and subsequently kill the wife that wants to come out of you. You never learned how to be a wife and for many, it's only a matter of time before the girlfriend role becomes evident again, as divorce looms in the near or far future, and you are right back where you started. Oooh, girl, that's a conversation for another time. Let's get back to the topic.

A boyfriend is a guy who doesn't fully understand how his authority works but will still operate in it prematurely and immaturely. If you think about it, a boyfriend is a mentality as well, and it is a guy that has also been misassigned. A man's process is to go from a **son** who then matures into **manhood** as he submits to his father's training (whether it be his natural father and/or his heavenly Father). That training develops him into a husband, and any role he accepts less than that, is a misassignment. A man is to assume his role as husband so that he may take a daughter and assign her the role of a wife. That way, she will always be a covered woman.

When a guy is immature, he will bring the woman **down** to his level and assign to her a role that is less than a wife. This level of immature dating is bursting at the seams because it is full of young men and women who don't know who they are or what they are doing. They still need to be fathered before being released as husbands and wives, and if they are released too soon, they will end up playing house instead of fulfilling their true purpose.

> " #TheGirlfriendTrap
>
> *If young men and women are released to date too soon before maturing into husbands and wives, they will end up playing house instead of fulfilling their true purpose.*
>
> #TheGirlfriendTrap "

You truly don't want to be at this level for many reasons, reasons that we are about to dive into headfirst. At this level, girls are confused and feel the desire to treat their boyfriends as husbands before developing as a wife. Guys are confused in the same way. They have the desire to exercise their authority over the woman, but they do so before actually being ready to be a husband to her.

When a guy calls you his girlfriend and you say "Yes," what you are really saying yes to is his immature leadership, his crime of stealing, and to a position of demotion and NOT promotion. You assume the role of a woman who is uncovered and confused, and it shows in the dynamic of the relationship every single time.

I was this girl, willing to be anything a guy wanted me to be as long as it meant I wouldn't spend another day feeling alone and abandoned. Now, *I sit as a daughter learning to be a wife,* watching girlfriends operate as immaturely as the boyfriends do. A girlfriend lets her boyfriend take charge over her as if she is legally his. She allows him to touch her in ways only a husband should touch his wife. She allows him to label and brand her with titles and gifts that show that she belongs to him, a cheap grab at ownership. But yet, she submits to it all. The dynamic of this kind of relationship breeds so much chaos; it ain't even funny.

If I could take a guess, 99% of the women I know who are girlfriends or who were girlfriends has taken some major blows to the heart and has lost a lot at some point in their life, crossing serious boundaries with guys. Let me ask you this question: Is it okay to have sex with your boyfriend? (Feel free to say your answer out loud). Is one slip-up no big deal? If you said yes to either of these questions, let me just say that the trap has been set, and it has already taken you hostage.

There is a way out, but first, you will have to identify the root cause of what made you walk into the trap in the first place. You will discover that the way you got into it will be the same way you will have to take to get out of it. So let's dive deeper into this girlfriend trap and uncover what the enemy of your soul so desperately tries to keep hidden in your life.

CHAPTER 5

The Trap Is Real

A trap is "a device or enclosure designed to catch and retain animals, typically by allowing entry but not exit." – Oxford's English Dictionary

Traps are designed to catch something with the hopes of it never getting free again. When you are trapped in something, you become very limited and restricted, never again being able to go about freely. Think of a bird, for example. Birds are created to fly to higher heights. It's their destiny. But when they fly into a trap, they are no longer able to fly. They can no longer go about doing their birdie thing and will never be able to reach those high heights again, assuming they never get set free.

The mindset of a girlfriend places you in a system that is designed to trap you. It is a system that constantly produces broken and fragmented women, preventing them from ever reaching the heights of their purpose and callings here on earth. These are women who go about life with holes in their soul, holes so deep that you can fit a whole human in it (figuratively speaking, queen, but you get what I'm saying).

But wait, think about that last statement. The hole is so big that she actually does try to fit a human in it, a guy. This prevents her from ever having a healthy marriage with this guy in the future because instead of being joined to him in holy matrimony, she instead engulfs him in her deep abyss of emptiness.

She will struggle to see any goodness in the things that God has called good because the different moving parts of this system have strategically broken her in that area. For example, if God says that He has prepared good men to cover his daughters in marriage, she will struggle to believe it because of the trashy behavior she has personally experienced as a girlfriend with immature boyfriends.

Here is another one: If God says that commitment is good, she will resent marriage and run away from it because of the "cheating" behavior she has experienced with boyfriends. Pause. Notice how I put cheating in quotations. This system is so calculated that it even makes women believe that the men they are with are theirs to even be cheated on in the first place.

She will be so fearful of marriage that she will begin to personally destroy her own chances of marriage to avoid it; something that this system has trained her to do. This system is designed to break you and keep you broken in faith and heart. It creates anger, bitterness, fear, regret, loneliness, desperation, and an idol worshiper within you. Yes, the ultimate ALL IN ONE package you never wanted.

The System of Sabotage

This system is called sabotage. It was designed with you and I (really ALL women) in mind. A system is a series of moving parts all working together to produce a desired outcome. You are more familiar with systems than you think. In fact, you are a system. All of your body parts work together as a unit to keep you alive so that you can function and do what you do on any given day. You have systems within that system. For example, your circulatory system, digestive system, endocrine system, immune system, etc.

Here is another example, the solar system, which we (earth) are a part of. It is a system of planets and stars that revolve around the sun which is designed to give life-sustaining light, heat, energy and many other things to us on earth. There are so many moving parts that go into a system that the human brain can't even understand it all. The same goes for this system of sabotage.

Within this system, there are many moving parts that are all functioning in your life, even now as you read this book. They are designed to sabotage your heart when it comes to love, sex and commitment. This system is so effective that it takes down generation after generation without them ever knowing what hit them.

To sabotage means to deliberately destroy, damage, or stop something from happening that is supposed to happen. This act of sabotage is usually carried out by an opposing party or an enemy of someone else's property. If you didn't know, you are the precious creation of God, and there is an enemy in motion that wants to destroy anything good that God has placed in you.

To go a little deeper, Online Etymology Dictionary describes the root meaning of sabotage as to walk noisily as with a wooden shoe. That kind of disruption is meant to "disturb the peace," and the true definition of peace is unity with God. So, when you become a part of this system, the enemy gets a 2-for-1 deal from your participation; no unity (peace) with a man and no unity (peace) with God. And unity with God is the most important unity you will ever have.

How does all this work? I am about to share with you some of the most amazing information that any young woman can know. It all starts with rejection.

Rejection

Since the fall of mankind in the Garden of Eden, the enemy (known as the devil) has worked tirelessly to make sure that mankind developed the same heart toward God that he has, and that is a heart of rejection. It's no coincidence that his first victim was a woman (Eve).

The woman (just like the man) is wired to accept good and healthy instructions from a figure of authority to carry out a mission. For the woman, one form of that instruction is DNA by way of a seed (sperm). That seed, when planted, gives birth to the most beautiful thing this earth has ever known, humans. When a human is born, her innate ability to nurture and nourish is put on full display as she tends to that human so that the cycle of creation and beauty can continue in the love of God.

The enemy deceived her and basically told her that she no longer needed God to be that woman. He told her that by disobeying God, she would be like God, and I would say, even better than God because she wouldn't create beautiful things and withhold them from her children like he insisted that God was doing to her when it came to the tree of the knowledge of good and evil. Check it out.

"Now the serpent was more crafty than any other beast of the field that the Lord God had made. He said to the woman, 'Did God actually say, You shall not eat of any tree in the garden?' And the woman said to the serpent, 'We may eat of the fruit of the trees in the garden, but God said, You shall not eat of the fruit of the tree that is in the midst of the garden, neither shall you touch it, lest you die.' But the serpent said to the woman, 'You will not surely die. For God knows that when you eat of it your eyes will be opened, and you will be like God, knowing good and evil.'" – **Genesis 3:1-5 (ESV)**

At that moment, he was teaching her to reject God and to have no boundaries or self-control. He was teaching her that all things that looked good to her were for her to consume if she so desired. He was teaching her to chase after what was not hers to have in the first place, and that same script is still being read and performed to this day.

She listened to him and rejected God. She didn't realize that what she was rejecting was God's heart for her and his instruction on how to live blissfully in a loving and committed relationship with Him. The enemy made it seem like she didn't need to accept ANY instructions but she ended up accepting his. Why? Because she was still a woman created to follow God's law and what that means is you will function how you are designed to, whether you receive and follow instruction for good or instruction for evil.

When rejection comes into your life, it acts like a cancer that spreads all over your body and won't stop spreading until every cell in you malfunctions. Rejection has to feed on itself in order to thrive. What that means is, it will always reproduce the same kind as it, in you and around you in order to stay alive. When you are rejected, it creates a wound in your soul that sets the tone for how you see yourself and thus how others see you.

Whatever is in your soul will always reproduce itself. What this looks like is you rejecting yourself and being rejected again and again with no end.

This repeated cycle of rejection, for the average young woman, looks like a life without Father God and/or a natural father, which is a life without a healthy authoritative figure to submit to, who will protect her and give her instruction and direction concerning her heart. It's a life where she unknowingly rejects herself. This almost always will end up with her being rejected repeatedly by guys.

The enemy's main goal all along was to remove the father from the life of a daughter and that's what happened with Eve. It may seem like God rejected her (and the man) by removing them from the Garden of Eden, but it was quite the opposite. Eve rejected God, her father, just like most women are doing today.

She rejected good instruction and by his law, she, along with the man, had to be removed from his immediate presence. When a woman rejects her father and removes him from his rightful position as such, it is a removal of a woman's covering, protection, instruction and direction in her life. These are all important things she needs to be a healthy, functioning woman, able to thrive in a committed relationship all while nurturing and nourishing the seeds she gives birth to, literally and figuratively.

The enemy has strategically removed fathers from the home today causing great and severe wounds of rejection in the souls of the children. He has removed them from their authoritative position as protector and instructor, creating broken daughters who are then forced to live with a gaping size hole in her soul that only a father can fill. Ultimately, the removal of the father is a result of generation after generation removing God as father in their lives and their offspring suffering from it and repeating the destructive cycle.

When a young girl grows up in search of a father's validation but never receiving it, she will go searching for it elsewhere. A father's authority is the highest authority in a daughter's life, and when it's not in place, she will inevitably search for any kind of an authoritative figure to fill that void and it's usually a knock-off version of her father.

This is a male that she will end up submitting to, whether she knows it or not because she is designed to be under a male covering. It is a deep longing for every woman, young and old, to have a man of authority in her life, and in this broken world, it feels like a thirst that seems impossible to quench. This is why women are so desperate to have a guy in their life in the first place.

This is all a part of the enemy's system of sabotage. He knows that your heart needs to be filled with a father's love from birth and without it, you would go searching to be covered by another "man" to fill that void. He knew that it would be one of the most intense pursuits you would ever embark upon which would be a sure way for you to easily walk into the trap and never get out.

What's the trap? **The trap is the guy making you his girlfriend, which makes you an uncovered woman,** as you ultimately never accept Father God or allow Him to cover you. And when you don't allow that to happen you prevent yourself from being filled and satisfied by His love and growing in that love. This will always result in perversion in your life, trapping you in sin, deceit, loneliness, confusion and outside the system of commitment and blessings.

Because you won't allow God to cover you and fill your voids, any guy that shows you any kind of attention will cause you to go into a dying desperation as your heart yells out "choose me, fill me." When a father is not in his rightful position in your heart, you are underdeveloped in areas like knowing your identity and being secure in it, following directions (order) and submitting to accountability, emotional stability, mastering the art of being content, discernment or knowing what to look for and how to choose a guy, recognizing true love and these are just a few areas.

If you are underdeveloped, a guy pursuing you romantically will break your heart even more because you will look to him to be your father instead of an equal partner. If you allow a man into your life anyway, you will open up your wounded, unhealed, heart to him in hopes of that gaping hole being filled. You will go out and try to fill that hole on your own and you will almost always try to fill it with a penis. You don't realize that your vagina and your soul or two different organs and a man's penis can't reach that far, nor does it have the power to fill or heal your soul. Your heart will now *live* in dying desperation as it screams out, "I need my father, please replace the missing ~~piece~~ peace in my life."

Rejection creates a deep void which then creates a desperation to fill that void. As you go searching for a man, you never seek the one who is truly able to fill your void, your heavenly father. You remain underdeveloped and ignorant of how to properly fill your voids and what it takes to have a healthy relationship with a guy. This causes you to misuse and abuse your body and the dynamic of a relationship, which then causes unfulfillment and being rejected all over again.

Wheeeeew, child talk about a system! And the crazy thing is, as the system of sabotage is in operation, there are smaller systems within that system that are at work simultaneously. Here are a few:

1. **The system of dishonor** – because you will have sex with the guy in hopes of trying to keep him. You dishonor both your body and his and your father's name, who never gave you away in marriage before having sex. This illegal sex keeps you uncovered and dishonored.

2. **The system of prostitution** – because you will be selling something of great value, yourself and true intimacy with God, in exchange for something of lesser value, like companionship and intimacy whose source is from a limited human. In reality, this kind of companionship and "fake" intimacy is limited and not fulfilling because it's void of God's love and presence.

3. **The system of infidelity and adultery** – because you will no longer see commitment as a requirement to be with you which will cause you to believe you don't need to be committed to God either. This also causes a disdain for the institution of marriage and gives birth to the #SideChickCulture in your life.

4. **The system of idol worship**-because you will learn to consistently put people and things before God, making them your god.

5. **The system of unbelief** – because of all the bad you will experience with guys and see others experience as well, you will no longer believe that God is good and loving as He says He is or is able to provide good things for you.

6. **The system of deprecation (disapproval of oneself)** – because you will no longer see yourself for how valuable you truly are. You will no longer believe you are worth anything more than how the previous or current guy is treating you, causing you not to understand the respect and honor God has attached to you.

Here is a diagram of the system of sabotage at work and rejection being the starting point. Notice, as long as the wound of rejection stays unhealed, the cycle continues. I purposefully used a triangle to depict this system to show you the high you feel as the arrows point up, only to come down to a crashing low to start back at rejection.

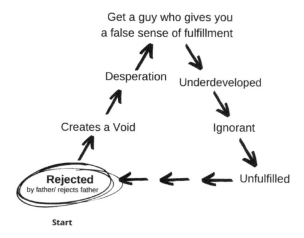

Let's have a moment of self-reflection. Examine your life and ask yourself if the system of sabotage is in full operation in your life. Just because your father is alive or even present physically does not mean he has affirmed and validated you emotionally and spiritually. It takes the full acceptance and the presence of God to make a healthy and whole young woman, and if your father has not accepted Jesus, then he does not fully know himself and is missing a key component in helping you develop. Rejection creates a lack of identity and there is no human walking on the face of the earth who has an accurate identity outside Jesus Christ, not one! Jesus is the full embodiment of the Father God, and when you don't know Father God, you don't know who you really are.

"Jesus said to him, 'I am the way, and the truth, and the life. No one comes to the Father except through me.'" – **John 14:6 (ESV)**

The system of sabotage was my life! I was on a merry-go-round and dying from the inside out, and I was completely unaware of it, all because I was rejected by my natural father. Because of that, I rejected Father God in return. Rejection breeds rejection.

I can't tell you how many women I know and see who are bound by this system. Unfortunately, many will never even desire to get out because it is the only mindset and way of living that they know. If you tell her anything different, she will look at you like you have 3 heads on your body.

Why do women marry this mindset? Simple, because it gets the guy...FAST. It's a false sense of satisfaction and fulfillment of that deep-rooted void of rejection, and I get it. Rejection is so painful that I totally understand why women settle for a guy to "fill" it even if it's not true fulfillment and unhealthy overall.

It's like having a deep wound, while being in excruciating pain, and grabbing for the quick relief of Tylenol, when in reality, what you really need is to undergo surgery. To go through a true healing process and to learn why you feel the way you feel and do the things you do takes time, "too long" of time for most women. It takes confronting the pain and like most people, they don't want to feel the pain, so they run from it and bury it deep. What I

#TheGirlfriendTrap

Out of sight does not mean out of heart. Until you address the wound, it will remain, festering as the days and years go by.

#TheGirlfriendTrap

have learned is that out of sight does not mean out of heart. Until you address the wound, it will remain, festering as the days and years go by.

If you keep overdosing on the quick relief of guys, you prevent or prolong your healing process, making your wounds worse at the same time. What you have been trying to find your whole life, God can give to you in an instant if you empty your heart and make room for Him. I know this to be true because he did it for me.

On top of that, culture tells you that you are nothing without a guy you can call your own, and with all that pressure you cave and give in. Ironically, the woman that pushes this same message has the same deep voids as you. She makes it seem like she has something you don't, but in actuality, she is using a guy to fill her voids just like every other young woman. She just hides it well until her life begins to crumble in public when she learns that "her man" can't fill her daddy wounds either.

The gravitational pull that the void of rejection has is so strong that the average woman can't live for too long without it being filled by something. And this is why I am pouring my heart and mind out to you during this girl chat. I want to tell you that the way you have been trying to fill this void doesn't work, and I want to show you how to fill this void in a healthy way so that you will never have to look to a guy to try to fill it (and fail at it) ever again. **I want to show you the path from being an uncovered woman to a covered daughter who properly sets herself up for true love, fulfillment and commitment.**

A part of that process is realizing that Father God loves you and accepts you. In fact, He has always loved and accepted you and has never rejected you. That truth alone is enough to bring healing to the heart of the hurt little girl in you who has been wanting to be wanted since conception. Now that you know Father God accepts you, you must learn to accept yourself. As truth comes in and your heart starts its healing journey, your view of self is going to need to be transformed and that only happens when you begin to think differently from how you thought before.

"Don't copy the behavior and customs of this world, but let God transform you into a new person by changing the way you think. Then you will learn to know God's will for you, which is good and pleasing and perfect." – **Romans 12:2 (NLT)**

Instead of thinking and behaving from a place of rejection, you can now start thinking and behaving like a fully accepted woman. The difference between a woman who lives and responds to life like a rejected woman vs. one who does not is her belief about herself. Although the journey of healing is just that, a journey, the biggest step is believing you are accepted by God. Once you take ownership of this truth, the cycle breaks and transformation begins to happen in your mind and in your life. Instead of the rollercoaster of emotions and the false sense of fulfillment, Father God will begin to bring to your heart everything that it so desperately needs, simply because you allowed Him into your heart and to accept you, and when you do that, you turn around and accept Him back.

Acceptance breeds acceptance and opens the door for healing and deliverance. It begins to tear the old mentality of girlfriend down so that you can build a new one, one of a committed woman, covered by God first and always, and a husband second if that is your desired path to travel.

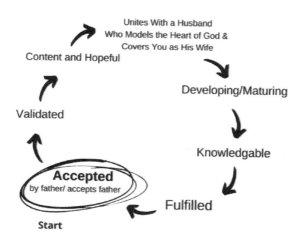

Every system ever created already has an end result, and if you want to become what God has called you to, then you will have to come completely out of this worldly dating system of boyfriend and girlfriend that has an end result of brokenness, sin, rejection and delay. God did not create this system, and He desires for you to step into his system of love and commitment.

The girlfriend system is designed to make you a *concubine,* but God's system is designed to make you a *committed* woman.

If you do this, you will no longer lose but gain open doors and blessings. I have explained to you **how** you got into this girlfriend trap and now I am about to explain to you **why** you are still in it and why it's been so hard for you to break free from it.

With any trap, there is bait. Bait is what a person uses to lure someone to the trap they've set. Think of cheese in a rat trap, but in this case, it's things that every young woman desires. Just like any trap, the bait used always appears to satisfy the one it's designed to trap, but once you get it, you soon realize you get more than you asked for. Let's talk about 3 baits that lure you to the girlfriend trap, 4 things that the trap creates and ultimately how to escape the trap and never get stuck in it again.

#TheGirlfriendTrap

The girlfriend system is designed to make you a concubine but God's system is designed to make you a committed woman.

#TheGirlfriendTrap

PART 2
The Bait & What the Trap Creates

CHAPTER 6

Bait #1 – Sense of Self-Worth

A sense of self-worth may seem strange that it's considered bait, but it's the perfect bait for any young woman who has any degree of low self-esteem. The average young woman has been flooded with worldly messages that teach her that if she doesn't have a guy to cuddle up with or claim as her own, then she is lacking in worth. Culture teaches you that somehow, if you have a guy, then his presence makes you better and more valuable, especially if he is good-looking or has a lot of money. Although this is a bald-headed lie and far from the truth, it's actually your perceived low value of yourself that lures you to the girlfriend trap, and once you get a boyfriend because of your low self-esteem, you think that your worth is in him and is now higher than it was without him.

This is a false sense of self-worth. There is nothing on this earth that can make you more valuable than you already are right now, and when you think less of yourself, you will accept less for yourself.

#TheGirlfriendTrap

When you think less of yourself, you will accept less for yourself.

#TheGirlfriendTrap

As a young woman, knowing your value is everything. It is the foundation to all healthy relationships, and it helps you to make the best decisions concerning your heart. To know your value means to know how much you are **worth** or the **importance** or **usefulness of yourself.** This simply means you know what's in you and how much it is worth. When you hear the word self-esteem, it is essentially the same as self-worth and it means to have an awareness of one's own value as a human. When someone says you have a low or high self-esteem, what they are saying is you consider your value to be really low or really high and it's based on how you see and treat yourself. Let's look at the word self-esteem a little more closely.

The word "esteem" means to estimate or to come up with a value for something. If someone were to give you a nice shirt and ask you how much you think it's worth, and you say $100, you just estimated that the value of that shirt is high, $100 worth! In other words, you are holding that shirt in high esteem. On the other hand, if you say 50 cents, well, then you hold it in low esteem, and its value, importance or usefulness, is not much to you!

I'm sure you have heard multiple times in your life that you must know your value or worth, and if you struggle with that concept, that's okay because I'm going to help you know yours today so that you will no longer fall for the bait of a FALSE sense of self-worth.

Another way to understand the concept of knowing your value is to ask yourself this question: What do I believe about myself? A belief is something that you see as truth and no matter what happens, no matter what the circumstances are, that truth does not change and remains the same.

So, tell me, queen, what do you believe about yourself? Do you believe that you are important? Beautiful? Intelligent? Honest? Loyal? A producer of good things? Worth someone else's or even your own time, money, effort and resources? Or do you believe that you are a mistake, not worth being seen or heard, ugly, dumb? One in a million instead of the one and only?

Some young women have never taken the time to really think about themselves in this way, and because of that, they allow themselves to be treated much lower than what their value requires. When you don't know the truth about yourself, you won't know how to see yourself or how to teach other people how to see you and treat you. Here is a truth I want you to always remember: What you believe about yourself determines how you see yourself, and how you see yourself determines how you treat yourself.

This also holds true when it concerns other people's view of you. Let's rephrase this so that you can see what I mean.

What you believe about yourself determines how OTHER people see you, and how OTHER people see you determines how they treat you.

How You See Yourself

A person can be the greatest athlete in the world, but if they don't see themselves for who they really are, they will never accept what they truly deserve and will never fulfill their potential in life. Can you imagine Serena Williams believing that she was a horrible tennis player and not worth the time of day? Me neither!

I decided a while back that I would never allow another guy to see me as his girlfriend or anything less than a covered young woman deserving the utmost care and respect. The first thing I did was begin to see myself for who I really am, a covered young woman deserving the utmost care and respect.

To start seeing yourself for who you really are, you have to start by acknowledging who made you. Check this out.

Then God said, "Let us make mankind in our image, in our likeness, so that they may rule over the fish in the sea and the birds in the sky, over the livestock and all the wild animals, and over all the creatures that move along the ground." – Genesis 1:26 (NIV)

Queen, do you see that? God made every human being in his image. That means you and I are a reflection of Him, and when people see us, they see God. It's kind of like when people see you they say, "wow you look just like your parents," except in this case, God's features are much better. (Sorry parents.)

As a young woman, you reflect everything that God is. That means you reflect his character, the distinct expressions of his heart. Some of the characteristics of God are: confident, excellent, joyful, whole, competent, suitable, desirable, integral, good, loving, committed, worthy, brilliant, beautiful, intelligent, powerful, authoritative, respectful, just, careful, honest, kind, creative, artistic, thoughtful, forgiving, gracious, selfless, courageous, funny, responsible, successful, considerate, generous, reliable, trustworthy, optimistic, compassionate, empathetic, patient, disciplined, authentic, humble, intentional, unique, wealthy, healthy and so much more.

There are so many great things about God that there are not enough words to describe just how amazing He truly is. Because God made you in his image, that means all of those good qualities are stamped onto you, and you reflect those good things just like the moon reflects the light of the sun at night. That means you can attach your name to all those traits. Let's practice. Insert your name below and read the following sentence out loud.

I, _____ am confident, excellent, joyful, complete, competent, suitable, desirable, integral, good, loving, committed, worthy, brilliant, beautiful, intelligent, powerful, authoritative, respectful, just, careful, honest, kind, creative, artistic, thoughtful, forgiving, gracious, selfless, courageous, funny, responsible, successful, considerate, generous, reliable, trustworthy, optimistic, compassionate, empathetic, patient, disciplined, authentic, humble, intentional, unique, wealthy, healthy and so much more.

Wow! How do you feel hearing yourself say all those good things about yourself? Do you feel important? Do you feel that all those qualities make you worth more than what you believed you were worth before? You should because what you have just done is establish your true value. You just spelled out what makes you important, useful and worth so much in this world. Giiiirrrrl, listen!!!

Important – significant, having high rank or status
Useful – capable of being put to use, having a purpose
Worth – the value of something measured by its qualities

I don't know about you, but I'm getting excited just thinking about all that goodness attached to my name, heeeeyyyyy! And get this, that's just the beginning of the list. There are sooooo many other great things about you that make your value shoot through the roof, and because you are so valuable, you can now see yourself in that way and act like it.

Your Value Never Changes

When God created you in his image, the very substance that makes up your frame is priceless, and truth be told, it can not even be measured by humans. You are made with the same substance that dwells in God. Read it for yourself:

"Then the Lord God formed a man from the dust of the ground and breathed into his nostrils the breath of life, and the man became a living being." – **Genesis 2:7 (NIV)**

This is the account of when God created the first human being. The very thing that humans are made of comes straight from God himself: Dust that he created with his hands and his very own spirit, which is the breath of life that he breathed into that dust. Although humans are not created like this today, it shows the valuable process of making the first human so that we can see that this value is embedded in us all no matter how we get here today, and it will never change.

Because his breath dwells within you, you can joyfully and rightly say that your value is out of this world and that you should be viewed and treated with the utmost respect no matter what you do, when you do it or whether you are aware of your value or not. Period! Because you come from God, you should be viewed with the same respect one views God.

Why do we respect God? Well, because He is the supreme being who created everything, who holds all the power, authority and love in existence. He has power over us and can do with us what He pleases, and so with knowing that, we view Him in the highest way possible because He embodies the best qualities there is. If we come from him, then that respect is on us too.

If you met the children of the president, would you treat them any kind of way? Most would not because of whom they are connected to. In no way am I saying excuse any bad behavior but what I am saying is respect the valuable. Since ALL humans come from God, then all humans are valuable and must be respected, specifically you, queen.

When you know that you are a valuable person, possessing God's qualities, and learning to walk in them and perfect them, it sets you apart from someone else who is equally valuable but does not know it. When you are aware of who you are, you will begin to act like who you are. Knowing that I have the ability to be honest, then actually living as an honest human makes my value more clear to those around me, and it increases my chances of elevation and gaining favorable opportunities.

Knowing what makes you valuable is key, and once you know it, you will respect yourself more and require others to respect you and everything that has to do with you. Your value as a human never changes, but it's those things that we are aware of that show our value and that's why it's crucial that you discover those things and never stop discovering those qualities about yourself.

Because God is respected, I am to be respectful and be respected by others. Because God is honest, I am to be honest and be told the truth by others. Because God is patient, I am to be patient and require others to be patient with me. Because God is committed to me, I am to be a committed person and require commitment from others if they want to engage with me concerning things that are valuable and cost a lot of my own time, care and effort.

It is my respect, patience, honesty and commitment that make me the valuable young woman that I am, and If I couldn't think of a single quality, being made in the image of God alone makes me extremely valuable.

When I began to see myself how God sees me, a reflection of Himself, I became so confident and sure of myself that I literally began to walk differently. I began to talk differently. I began to dress differently, #HolyBootyAndBreast. I interact with guys differently now, and let me tell you, queen, NOBODY can tell me ANYTHING different about myself. It would just be a waste of good clean air coming out of their mouth.

It's these qualities within me that make me valuable, and that makes every *relationship* I have with another human that much better. It's these qualities in me that make every organization or community I become a part of that much better. What that means is, once I become a part of your life or organization, your life or organization becomes better because of me. I don't make another person valuable; only God gives true value, but my presence makes what we share together better. Yes, and the same goes for you too. Believe it!

I am a queen. I am royal, and when you come from a royal bloodline (God's of course), it is a must that you be treated as such. The same goes for you. I have been calling you queen this whole time because that's how valuable and royal you really are.

Now that you have a better understanding of your value, it's your responsibility to position yourself in a way that commands the royal treatment that you deserve, yes, I said deserve.

This is not arrogance, conceit nor deceit; this is #FACTS. If God said it, then you have to believe it no matter what situation you are currently in or how much change is happening around you. If you struggle to believe this, it's because you have allowed culture to devalue you and have adapted to the low standards that women have held for so long. It's time out for that.

When something is of a high value, you can't just treat it in any kind of way. Have you ever paid a couple of hundreds or even thousands of dollars on an item? If so, do you let everyone and their momma do whatever they want to do with it? Of course not! I hope not! When something is valuable, you set it apart from all the other things to preserve the things about it that make it so valuable or high priced. To help you set yourself apart, I'm going to give you an example of how people treat something that they see as extremely valuable in this world...an original masterpiece.

Original Masterpiece

A masterpiece is a piece of art that is considered the best of its kind or the greatest piece from that particular artist. Not only is it the best but it's also the original. You can't have multiple original masterpieces because there's literally only **one** original masterpiece. Even if you make a mass reproduction of it, it'll only be a copy or an imitation of the original.

Where can you find these masterpieces? Can you go to your local store and find them on the shelf? No! These original masterpieces are sold for millions and millions of dollars, a very high value. They are in one place, one country, one state, one exhibit, and when you go to see it, it's not easily accessible. You can't just walk up to it and touch it. Usually, they're either up high out of reach or locked up in this really big casing.

Why is that? To keep people away from it to prevent damage. Think about it; if anyone were able to go up and touch it with their crummy, oily fingers, it would be ruined, leaving oil stains and marks all over it. It's lifted up high from the general public for its own protection.

I want you to begin to look at yourself as that original masterpiece because that's what you are. One master and great artist created you just as you are, beautiful, with every color, texture and stroke carefully thought out beforehand. You are valuable, unique and the only one of its kind. Really, think about yourself for a second. There is no one in the world like you. Even if you have an identical twin, you two are not completely identical. You are 2 totally different people with qualities that make you unique individuals.

Because you are unique, because you are a masterpiece crafted with so much effort and detail, because your estimated value is so high, you should be kept out of the public's reach to prevent damage and to preserve the beautiful qualities that you have that make you so valuable. No one should have easy access to you and there should be special requirements to get close to you.

Just like that masterpiece, there is only one of its kind and the price is astronomical. Even so, there is always a buyer who recognizes its worth and is willing to pay the price for it to admire the beauty, hardwork and the story that comes with it, and maybe brag about it a little. If a masterpiece that's an inanimate object, that's not as nearly as valuable as you can be treated with so much importance and care, why are you not treating yourself with even greater importance and care?

How does a young woman do that? Simple, she positions herself in a way that sets her apart from things that would be considered of low value. Let's learn the difference between these 2 words, common and uncommon.

Common Vs. Uncommon

Common means:

1. To be widespread.
2. To be easily accessible.
3. Something that's available to the public, meaning anyone can have it or use it.
4. Belonging to two or more people.
5. Lack of special privilege.

What are some common things in life? How about your popular grocery store? That's very common. I'm sure you can find one close by no matter where you live these days. What about your most popular fast-food restaurants? It can be a brand of shoe or maybe it's your favorite pair of jeans or a cute shirt. You get my drift, right? Common is anything that you can just go pick up at the store or on the corner. Anyone can have it.

But what about you? Can you be found anywhere?

Take myself for an example. There's only one Brittany. You can't find me in every state in the United States. You can't find me in Africa nor in Australia. You can't even find me down the street. You can only find me right here, right now. You may find many people with the name Brittany Jones, but there's only one Brittany Jones with my character, my looks, my personality...me. This is the same for you too.

You are not common, and the reason why I say that is because there is only one YOU! You're not easily accessible, and no one can just go and pick you up anywhere they go. That leads me to the definition of uncommon.

Uncommon means:

1. Extraordinary or above the ordinary
2. Rare
3. Unusual, meaning you're not the norm.

Although the things that make you valuable can be found in other masterpieces (people), when they are placed in you, that makes you completely different from other masterpieces. One artist can make 2 different masterpieces and use the same colors and similar designs on both. But those same characteristics placed on 2 different canvases make them into 2 completely different pieces of work.

Jessica and Jackie both are brilliant, funny and kind, but those characteristics are expressed differently through Jessica than they are through Jackie, making them unique individuals. What I am saying here is, because of who you are and what you possess, you have the privilege of placing yourself in a position that's hard to reach. Not only do you have this privilege, but I consider it foolish if you don't use that privilege for your own benefit. Why? Because what you value the most, you protect the most.

If you see yourself as someone with low value, so will others. When a guy sees you as a low value and common young woman, he will see you as easily

What you value the most, you protect the most.

#TheGirlfriendTrap

accessible, available to the public, potentially belonging to him or other guys with no requirements and unlimited access. I don't know about you, but I approach common things much differently than I do things that are valuable and uncommon. When it is common, I know I can always go and get another one. But when it is a masterpiece, I respect it to the highest degree. I wouldn't want to be the one to mess it up in any way.

The role of a girlfriend carries no substantial weight on the earth, and because of that, the general public treats this role as something less than. Why? Because it is less than, less than the legit role of a wife that God created for you. This girlfriend role that women assume is so cheap and common that you can easily become one, be had as one, whether it be for a year or for a day, be dumped as one, and nobody gives a dang about it after it's all said and done. It's as if your role as that girlfriend never existed, and if you become the girlfriend to another guy, the cycle will repeat itself all over again.

A girlfriend is easily accessible, available to the public and will potentially belong to 2 or more guys in her lifetime. There are no special requirements to have her, and there is unlimited access to her, like a rollercoaster at an amusement park. It doesn't take much to ride her as long as she opens the gate to let you in. It's the girlfriend way.

To no longer fall for this bait, you have to understand your value in God and stand on it! Or else you will always measure your value based on a guy in your life and be miserable for the rest of your life.

Girlfriend Confession #1

Early on as a girlfriend, I had no clue of just how unique and valuable I was. If a guy liked me, then I would give him a chance, a chance to have me whenever he wanted me. I was just glad to be wanted. I was so desperate for the affection of a guy that even if he just wanted my body in sex, I interpreted that as wanting me as a person. I thought they were one and the same.

I kept giving him my body just so that he wouldn't leave me because I didn't see anything valuable about me to keep him! In my eyes, I was cheap and as common as can be and the fact that he chose me made me feel special. I equated him choosing me as making me more valuable in some way. My low self-esteem was what kept me in the trap.

My thought was, if he wasn't getting it from me, then he was going to get it from someone else. I know you've heard the same thing, right? So, I made sure that I was on the bottom shelf, not requiring much effort to reach me. I just couldn't afford for him to pass me up and move on to the next girl who could offer him more than me.

I wore my low self-esteem like underwear, not seen but always there. When you risk your life, by sneaking him over in the middle of the night, knowing that your mother was just in the other room with the power to end both his life and yours if caught (laughing but very serious), just to make sure he was pleased so that he would keep coming back to you, that's low self-esteem.

I couldn't see that I was already valuable whether he wanted to talk to me or not, so valuable that I could have required him to rise up to the standard that my value demanded instead of stooping down so low and actually allowing him to tell me my worth. Isn't it amazing how much power we give guys over us? Amazingly scary! When you let another human tell you your value, they will always lowball you. They can't give value to what they didn't create.

> #TheGirlfriendTrap
>
> *When you let another human tell you your value, they will always lowball you. They can't give value to what they didn't create.*
>
> #TheGirlfriendTrap

*** **Do you have a girlfriend story/confession that you want to share? I would LOVE to hear it. Text me your age and confession at 708-580-8823**

How to Let Go of the Bait: Know Your Value

God never creates duplicates, and he always places the best features in his creations which make them extremely valuable. Let me say it again: You are valuable, and there is NO ONE on this earth that can be you or do it like you can!! * 2 snaps up.

Let go of the bait of this false sense of self-worth by knowing what truly makes you valuable. Write out everything that makes you valuable. I mean from what you look like, the gifts and talents you have, to the things that make you weird and stand out. Every detail about you is like color and texture added to the masterpiece that you are, and it ALL adds up to make you the high-priced girl that you are.

Don't worry, there's plenty of qualities about you that make you valuable! I started a list of what I believe makes me valuable. Feel free to copy mine, along with the character traits we described earlier in the chapter. This will help you start your list, and don't you dare hold anything back.

What Makes Me Valuable

1. I am created by God
2. I am a woman
3. My ability to give birth to humans
4. My brown beautiful skin tone
5. My natural kinky hair and my fun and vibrant hairstyles that I create
6. All of my facial features
    a. My beautiful smile
    b. My brown eyes
    c. My imperfect skin
7. My height (5' 1" and just right)
8. My faith in Jesus and desire to live by His word
9. My pursuit of integrity
10. My honest heart
11. My ability to be selfless
12. My crazy laugh
13. My fitness and health
14. My kindness
15. My gentleness
16. My patience
17. My "Turn up "capabilities
18. My awkwardness and funny facial expressions
19. My gift of exhortation
20. My gift of teaching
21. My desire to learn
22. My unique fingers and toes
23. My empathy for others
24. My love for animals
25. My cleanliness and organizational skills
26. My personality
27. My loyalty and faithfulness
28. My communications skills
29. The scars on my body
30. The permanent retainer that I have

What Makes Me Valuable

Okay! Now it's your turn. Write out what makes you valuable.

CHAPTER 7

Bait #2 – Easy Access

Easy Access is a bait that gets you into the girlfriend trap because you love the fact that you can get the company of a guy in an instant. This is what you have always wanted, for someone to be there for you. You can text and call him instantly and at any time you want to. You can spend time with him whenever you want. The thing is, it's a healthy desire to want someone to be there for you at any moment, but unfortunately, what a boyfriend does is only "appear" to fulfill that desire, and most of the time, it's short-lived.

There is a difference between someone being easily accessible and someone being available to you. Boyfriends are easily accessible, but they are not available, and availability is what you truly desire. Although you can touch him and it feels like you are getting everything you have always wanted from a guy with no hindrances: accessibility, or his presence alone, does not equate to real long-term love, joy, satisfaction, being seen and heard, and having someone that will be there for you no matter what: availability.

That initial thrill of you getting the guy makes it feel like your voids and emptiness are finally being fulfilled, making you so excited, but in reality, they are not, because a boyfriend does not have the proper tools or "know how" to truly satisfy your heart how it needs to be satisfied. We will talk more about that in the chapter about false expectations.

Because a boyfriend is so easy to access, as a woman, you subconsciously make yourself easily accessible to him. In a way, it's you telling the guy, "thank you for being there for me, now I give myself to you in any way you want as a reward."

Low self-esteem plays a major role in that way of thinking. When we believe that something has less value or no value at all, we make it easily accessible, including ourselves.

I have discovered that in these boyfriend-girlfriend relationships, easy access is the most "enticing" bait a girl grabs ahold of. While he may be accessible to you, it's the perfect set-up to make yourself too accessible to him and dishonor, and not protect yourself in the process. Your accessibility to him goes unchecked, and there simply is no way to check it because the boyfriend-girlfriend dynamic breeds easy access and does not require any boundaries. It seems like a good idea to bite this bait but let me show you how this bait messes you up more than any other bait in the trap. Let's go back to the masterpiece example.

When anyone and everyone has access to that original masterpiece, some kind of destruction is right around the corner. Say, for instance, the owner of that masterpiece allows you to take it home just to try it out to see how it looks with your furniture. Mind you, you did not pay for it, yet and it's worth millions of dollars. They take it down from its high protected place, and they help you try to fit it into your car. In the process, you scratch the side of it trying to get it through the back car door. You settle for stuffing it into the trunk with the top open and ropes tied around it so it won't fall out while you are driving.

You finally get it home and accidentally drop it on the driveway pavement, denting the corner of the frame. As you walk it into your house, a little kid, not paying attention, runs past it while accidentally kicking the bottom front part of the picture, leaving a very visible dent. This makes the picture look a little distorted, but hey, it's not like you paid for it; why be upset about it? As you figure out where to hang it, the dog comes by and marks his new territory, if you know what I mean.

Wow! Despite all of that, you find a place, take a nail and hammer it into the wall. As you attempt to hang the masterpiece, you miss the nail, allowing the entire piece to hit the floor but not before it catches the corner of the mantle on the fireplace, creating a nice size two-inch tear right in the middle of it from the back.

You realize that you don't want the piece after all; it doesn't really match your decor so you take it back to the museum. But there is just one problem. It's not in its original condition anymore. It has endured injury and loss! The museum tries to restore as much of it as possible but not without evidence that injury has occurred. This original masterpiece is not looking so "original" anymore.

This beautiful masterpiece is you as you lend yourself out and become so easily accessible to a guy(s) to see if you are good enough to keep.

Lights...Camera...Access

You are born into this world wanting and waiting to be loved, to be nurtured and nourished, to be taught how to act as a girl growing into womanhood and how to be treated as one. You learn about romance and love through books, movies, music and even watch the relationships around you, hoping that one day, that would be you. In the movies, the girl gives herself to the guy and somehow she always gets him in the end. She does all the things a girlfriend in today's culture would do: touch, kiss, have sex, and after some kind of conflict, they makeup and get back together. We imagine after the movie is over that they are real people somewhere having their 3rd child in a hidden love nest.

"Wow! I want that," you think, as those seeds begin to take root and grow in your heart.

"If it worked for her, then it has to work for me too. Right?"

So you borrow this scene and begin to act it out as you prepare for your audition for the girlfriend role that you have been waiting all your life to get. Lights... camera...access! You find the first guy that you think is cute or cute enough, and you let him in, into your thoughts and your fantasies. Into your ears as he begins to tell you everything your father never did.

"I Love you baby girl. I'm going to be with you through whatever. I will protect you. You are so beautiful. What do you need? Don't worry about it, I will buy it."

Into your personal space through hugs and touch that send weird, yet stimulating feelings all throughout your body. You can't help but want to feel it again and again as curiosity gets the best of you as you wonder how the rest of his body will make you feel. Into your heart, as you become emotionally attached to him, and your desires become fixated on anything that has to do with him. Into your clothes, where he can see everything that even the sun doesn't have the privilege to gain access to. And ultimately into your body, a place that was never meant to be entered into by just anyone, but only the one who knows just how valuable it is, never wanting to harm it in the slightest way.

Access means to gain entry to, to give one permission to come in and do as they choose. When you let someone into your home, for example, you give them the chance to go into whatever part of the house they want to. You can lock doors and tell them that certain areas are off-limits, but if they wanted, they can break in some kind of way.

This is the same with your heart except there are no locks to pick, just open doors; doors you didn't even know existed. You can say all day long that you are not going to let him into certain areas of your heart, but the heart moves to its own beat. It tends to take the wheel and drive where it will get the most satisfaction, even if its final destination is off a cliff. It tends to leave you in the back seat, able to see every street and turn but never giving you the power to take control of the wheel to change direction.

Everything we do comes from the heart, and that's why we are commanded by God to protect it at all times.

"Above all else, guard your heart, for everything you do flows from it." – **Proverbs 4:23 (NIV)**

Once something gets in, you realize that it's not that easy to tell it to leave. When you give a guy access to your heart, you give him the power to change things around, to bring things in and even steal things.

Romanced Robbery

I hear songs that make it seem cool to be in relationship after relationship, and how they learned from each one as if what they experienced was actually good for them. I guess this is the "experience" the young girl was referring to from the introduction. Usually, experience sets you up for an advancement, to actually get a job or position. And yes, you do learn things from being in different relationships, but it's mostly things of what not to do, and most people are not that aware in the relationship to even make that connection.

The majority of the experience that you gain takes more from you than it deposits in you, draining the good qualities you have instead of strengthening them for the next opportunity. Why is this so? Because our hearts are not resumes that only hold on to good things that have happened to it. It's a memory bank that keeps a record of all things, and the bad generally overrides the good. That young lady may see this as experience, but I see it for what it really is: robbery! Let's call it romanced robbery to be exact.

When you give a guy access to you, who has no intention of staying, you unlawfully give him things he should not have, and he unlawfully takes it from you because whatever you put in his hands, whatever part of you he got a hold of when he was with you, he takes with him when he leaves. Let's break down the idea of robbery so you can understand exactly what I am saying here.

Rob – "to remove valuables from a place unlawfully" – **Merriam-Webster Dictionary**

Steal – "to take (another person's property) without permission or legal right and without intending to return it" – **Oxford English Dictionary**

Theft – "the taking of another person's property or services without that person's permission or consent with the intent to deprive the rightful owner of it." – **Wikipedia**

This is why nobody is super-excited when they break up. You feel a pain, a ripping apart, a loss that leaves you low and dry with no one to call on for help. This is the most cold-blooded robbery I believe there is, because it's one that numbs all of your senses before it happens, making sure that your guard is completely down as you daydream and plan out how many of his babies you are going to have in the future. And then it happens right before your googly eyes as you willingly forfeit the things that make you valuable. And what might that be?

Integrity

Your virginity is not a burden, nor is it a bargaining tool. It's a precious gift that is attached to a very important characteristic that you have, and you are the only one who has the power and privilege to give it to someone else. Ooh, I LOVE that!

It is to be cherished and protected from harm and abuse, but once you give it unlawfully, and he takes it unlawfully, it is one thing lost that you won't be able to get back.

> #TheGirlfriendTrap
>
> *Your virginity is not a burden, nor is it a bargaining tool.*
>
> #TheGirlfriendTrap

Having sex as a girlfriend, and not as a wife, robs you of your sexual integrity. Integrity...that's the valuable characteristic that sex is attached to, and it's the state of living in truth and wholeness and not in a lie or division. When you have sex with a guy you are not married to, you give up your power to live a life of truth. Let me explain.

Sex is an act of commitment. It's an act the speaks loudly without words and what sex says is, "I am with you until death do us part. I am committed to you." When you have sex with someone, you are telling them that you are committed to them and them only. Well, if you did not actually commit your life to them in marriage, (because marriage is the only kind of commitment there is between a man and woman), you are lying to them. You are doing something with your body that you did not do with your heart, your life.

And get this, you are not only lying to them, but you are lying to yourself and all those around you. To live a life of sexual integrity (telling the truth with your body) shows your ability to commit and remain faithful to one person. When you have sex outside of commitment, it works against you because you are showing that you are a liar and that you don't know how to be committed and be faithful to one person, since you are not committed to the person you are having sex with right now.

Do you see how that works? You are lying to him, and if someone considered marrying you, they would have the right to ask this question, "You have had sex with this guy (and that guy), how do I know you won't have sex with another guy while you are married to me?"

Hmm! That's a really good question. How would he know? Since you have no real standards regarding who you have sex with, what's going to stop you from cheating in your marriage if all this time you have made it a practice to lie and have sex with whoever you choose to?

What are the requirements for you to have sex with a guy? Your current actions will tell you. Does all a guy have to do is be your boyfriend? Show you some attention? Buy you something big or small? If yes, many guys can and will do that for you, and that's all it will take to get you in the bed.

" #TheGirlfriendTrap

If commitment is not the standard to have sex with you, then it won't take much to get you to have sex outside of it.

#TheGirlfriendTrap "

If commitment is not the standard to have sex with you, then it won't take much to get you to have sex outside of it. Since you are lying as a girlfriend (unmarried woman) you will lie as a wife (married woman). This makes you an untrustworthy person. And the same goes for boyfriends who are having sex. It creates a cracked and flawed foundation in any relationship.

When you have sex as a girlfriend, you allow yourself to be robbed of the opportunity to give your husband a gift that no one else has ever had before...you. You are robbed of the ability to give your husband the privilege of not being compared to anyone else's sexual abilities. You also rob yourself of the gift of sexual satisfaction as dis-contentment will grow as you compare your husband to your previous sexual partners.

Differences in sexual ability will always exist among people, and you'll be more satisfied if you don't have past experiences to distract you from potentially greater ones with him.

Although there is an argument for premarital sex, sex outside a committed marriage is never a gain. It's not "training," or an opportunity to become better at it in hopes of being the greatest sex partner your husband has ever had. You will have time to perfect your skills while you are married, and there's no need to rush. When it comes to premarital sex, you lose more than you gain, and if you ask me, it's too much to lose.

Trust (In Men)

Now, let me show you how a lack of integrity affects your heart and your ability to trust. As we have previously established, men are created to be protectors. They are to protect women from hurt, harm and danger, and we as women should be able to trust them to do that. We develop this kind of trust toward men through healthy relationships with fathers, brothers, uncles and friends.

When you give a guy access to your heart, specifically through sex, and he fails to commit to you before the act even happens, that trust is shattered before it ever had a chance to be built. With every act of sex is a promise given that vows to honor and protect you, provide for you, cherish you, never leave you and never forsake you. When a man makes this promise to you with his body but doesn't do it with his life in marriage, he straight up lies to you.

This is the other side of the coin that we don't think about. You become bitter in your attitude towards him, and really, men in general, and it happens on a subconscious level.

Like my brother-in-law told me, you don't have to be conscious of the act for your body to receive it in its intended form. That means you don't have to be aware that this guy is lying to you for your soul to receive and recognize the lie.

You then begin to rack up a list of more guys who hurt and lied to you than protected you. You will begin to expect bad behavior from men which in turn will put you on guard, turning you into a young woman that you never wanted to be: assuming, snooping, anxious, paranoid, and in fear that what happened before will happen again. Instead of building yourself up, you focus your attention on making sure another guy doesn't tear you down. This is a life of fear, tormenting fear.

> " #TheGirlfriendTrap
>
> *You don't have to be conscious of the act for your body to receive it in its intended form.*
>
> #TheGirlfriendTrap "

This is no way to live, and it takes away your freedom to be joyful with hopeful expectations. This is also unfair to the person you will spend the rest of your life with because he will now have to fight you just to get to the real you. That's if you choose to do the work to even make it to him in the first place. He will have to drill into the callous heart that has developed due to all the previous hurt that you've experienced in the hands of other guys; guys who should have never had access to you in the first place. You become so callous that you will talk yourself out of the real relationship that you were created for as it will no longer be appealing to your wounded heart.

Confidence (or Self-Esteem)

I can't even begin to tell you how true this is. When you give yourself at a discounted price, you teach yourself that you are not worth the wait, or commitment. You teach yourself that you are not worth working for or investing in. This causes you to see yourself differently and allow yourself to be treated as less than your masterpiece value.

For example, after giving your body away for the first time, it becomes easier to do it again and again. The shyness and even shame of showing your private parts to a guy become less and less, and what was always supposed to be private goods eventually becomes public property. Have you ever wondered why you even feel the sense to cover up or feel shame in showing your body to your boyfriend in the first place? I wholeheartedly believe that those are God-given internal signals that tell you that it's not safe to expose yourself to a guy who is not your husband. A man who doesn't have the right to have you will be spiritually blinded to your true beauty and worth anyway. To him, your body is just a thing of pleasure and a fun time. These internal signals protect you from doing it again.

To be treated less than what you are worth does damaging things to your subconscious mind, which in turn causes you to settle for less...and less. Let me ask you a few questions.

Have you ever said that you would never be something and then look up after some time and find that you have become the very girl you said you would never be?

"Wow! When did I start to feel that it was okay to be one of many? To be a side piece, or a piece of myself at all? When did I start letting him call me out of my name? When did I start to feel proud to be at the top ...of the bottom? Well, at least, I'm the main chick. He may talk to her but he comes home to me."

O ye of little esteem.

Or how about this one.

Was there ever a time that you were so sure of yourself? Anything you put on you felt you looked good in, right? You never felt the need to compare yourself or try to look better than the next girl. Until he made a comment, "you need to look more like her," or "I don't like this about you, be like this instead." The more you let guys in to tell you what they like, the more you change, trying to be everything he, he and he likes, losing yourself and the ability to determine what you like. Some of us even begin to start competing with other women just to keep his attention.

You forget who you are, hurrying to get the fake hair and plastic body to try and keep up with other women who have lost their identity and self-esteem too. **You forget that you are that original masterpiece that was already approved before going out on display.** You forget that you were not called to this earth to please men but to reflect God in Heaven who created you as you are, whether he, he or he likes it or not. You forget that you were never created to be fake and plastic but to bring others into self-love using your very real flaws and imperfections. Slowly but surely, the confident girl you once were has now become insecure of her wardrobe, her personality, her beautiful, natural body and features.

The more access you give to a guy(s), the easier it becomes to deface the masterpiece that you are. Queen, don't gloss over what I just said there. Even just one guy that has gotten too close to you can do the harm of many guys if he is the wrong guy or even the right guy but is immature and premature. The more you trust a guy or believe that he is the one, the more hurt you will feel if you are wrong. Only time will show a person's true character, and you don't want to let anyone into your personal space before knowing who they really are. The effect this kind of behavior has on you is lifelong.

It will be like having a very expensive electronic device and then scratching it, again and again. The next time you scratch it, you will think:

"Oh! I don't care. It was already messed up anyway."

Over the course of your life, you will lose your sense of honor and desire to protect yourself from harm, and that's a dangerous state to be in.

Girlfriend Confession #2

Every guy that I talked to, I gave access to in some way. I didn't know what boundary lines were, so I had none. I was always open, willing and able like a puppy waiting at the door for its owner to come home. No matter the time of day, sunup to sundown, if there was an opportunity for us to be together, I took it.

You always hear, "don't open the door for strangers," but with guys, I saw it differently. If he showed interest in me, I wasn't about to pass up on a chance to feel wanted, so I let him in. I didn't know him. I didn't have a gauge to measure him by to make sure he was worth my time or not, or even if he was just a stone-cold predator coming in to rob me silly. Sometimes, it took a few conversations, and for others, a fine face and a nice smile. I gave him access to my heart, letting him into the room of hope.

"I hope he wants me more. I hope he loves me. I hope he won't leave me. I hope he can replace the love my father never gave me."

Then I let him into the room of trust.

"I trust you with my feelings, make me happy. I trust you with my time, consume it. I trust you with my body, have it."

When I gave him access to my body, I never realized just how serious it was. I let him in to change the condition of my physical health if he wanted to. He could have brought as many diseases that he could carry, and I would have never known. I let him in to change my status from single woman to single mother if he wanted to, never thinking twice about the life I would be forced to adapt to as I raise my children without a present father.

I gave him access to my possessions, my precious time that I will never get back, sensitive information about me and so much more. It was all in hopes of me getting a FOREVER partner in return that would love me forever no matter what. Boy, was I in for a reality check! The worst pain that I experienced was giving him access to all of me, only to watch him walk away with it in the end. Talk about feeling robbed.

*** Do you have a girlfriend story/confession that you want to share? I would LOVE to hear it. Text me your age and confession at 708-580-8823

How to Let Go of the Bait: Put Boundaries in Place

Although a boyfriend seems so easily accessible, what your heart truly desires is real and authentic availability, not just physically, but emotionally and spiritually.

Switch out this bait for the real thing by protecting your heart and shredding the ALL access pass you have been handing out. Determine what kind of access you are willing to give a guy whom you are interested in but not married to. You never want to walk into anything blind and without a strategy on how to protect and preserve yourself from hurt and or injury. The saying by Benjamin Franklin definitely holds true, "When you fail to plan, you plan to fail."

***Healthy Tip: Only allow access to things that will not change your physical, emotional and spiritual condition permanently, or that you don't mind giving away or losing if he has access to it and walks away. The goal is to become a pro at guarding your heart so that you can position yourself to have the best and healthiest relationship in the future. I have created my own list as well. Feel free to use it to help build yours or even copy it for yourself. To find out WHY I chose what I chose, keep reading.

He *CAN* have access to	He *CAN NOT* have access to
1. My trusted family and close friends 2. "Get to know me" conversation	1. My body in sex 2. My body in intimate touch, like kissing and rubbing 3. Alone time 4. Acts of favor = washing, cooking, grooming, etc. 5. Intimate info about me 6. My money 7. My car 8. My bedroom 9. Private/nude pictures 10. Night time hours

Access

1. **Family/friends** – I need all eyes, ears and wisdom on deck to help me make the best decisions concerning this guy, like if I should walk away or take the next step with him toward commitment. I allow others in that I trust because they will be able to see things that I can't due to my infatuation with him.

2. **Conversation** – Talk, talk, talk! I want to get to know him, and he needs to get to know who I am, what I'm looking for and what I'm not looking for. Truthful conversation (along with God's guidance) will let me know if this is the guy for me or not. Ya girl ain't down for no secrets nor surprises. If he's crazy, I'll find that out before he does about himself.

No Access

1. **Body (sex)**: Sex is a permanent act with permanent consequences. It changes your physical, emotional and spiritual conditions in a permanent way. It creates a bond between the two involved that if broken, causes severe hurt and damage to your entire being. I am reserving this act for the one who is committed to me so that we both can reap the benefits from it and not a loss from misusing it.

2. **Body (intimate touch)**: You can not control the chemical hormones released in your body that create bonds through touch. You can only respond to them. One example is Oxytocin. This bonding hormone is released during intimate touch, like kissing, and it also causes you to trust the person more and let your guard down. This clouds your judgment and the ability to see a person for who they really are, which is not good at all. It's also an act of foreplay; play that gets your body ready to have sex. Since I'm not having sex, I don't want to start that engine.

3. **Alone time**: The number one way to break every boundary, especially the sex boundary, is to find yourself alone with the opposite sex. Pride tells you that you are strong enough to handle or resist any temptation that may pop up. But wisdom will tell you that temptations are not made to fight with but to flee from. Temptations come in with the hope to kill, steal and destroy you and whatever goals you have. They have more stamina than you and

will eventually wear you out and pin you down for the count. I refuse to set myself up for a fall.

4. **Acts of favor**: Favor is the help that promotes the personal growth, comfort and advancement of someone, and only when a guy finds (obtains) me as his wife, will he gain access to these acts of favor.

5. **Intimate info about me**: This is info that if withheld, will not interfere with his judgment of my character or assessment of me as a woman whom he could possibly see himself committing to. There are some things about me that I won't just share with anyone. Everyone does not know how to handle all my complexities and insecurities, and I need to feel safe in order to share them. Commitment or the promise to commit will provide that safety.

> ***Healthy tip:** Only share info that you wouldn't mind being told to anyone else because if he walks away, he is taking with him whatever you gave him access to, and he can do whatever he wants with that info.

6. **My money/car**: Outside of willingly giving gifts of kindness, there is no giving him my money to do anything, my name to sign off on anything, or my car to drive at his leisure. Exchanging gifts can be a slippery slope, and I talk more about that in my book, *35 Tips on How to Win at Dating,* shameless plug. Go to SheAbundantly.com and be ready to buy it when it's available to the public. When it comes to giving guys things, I learned the hard way (very hard way) that if a guy does not have his own, he doesn't need a woman right now. He needs a strategy on how to grow up.

> ***Healthy tip**: Let a boy grow up to be a man or become his momma! #Facts

7. **My bedroom/private pics**: My bedroom is where I undress and have my most private moments. My body is private goods, now devoted to the God who created it and the man who will commit to cherish it. I don't allow guys into those spaces because it's simply not for them to see. They are exclusive territory meaning if you don't have the status of a husband, you can't get in. Exclusivity creates a longing and desire to want in. It also creates a

challenge that guys desperately want and need when it comes to pursuing you, and it sets a young woman apart from the rest, making her even more attractive. If she is not giving guys access to private places, it increases the safety and trust that a guy will place in her later on.

8. **Night-time hours:** Again, exclusivity! Unless we are with family or out in group settings having fun, he's just going to have to catch me during the day. There will be no late-night creeping. This eliminates any temptations or traps that would have presented themselves otherwise. Imagination is the only visual he will have of me at night.

Okay! Now it's your turn. You can do this girl! You are worth EVERY Boundary. Be honest with yourself and remember it's okay to protect yourself at all costs.

He *CAN* have access to	He *CAN NOT* have access to

To help secure your new boundaries, write a few sentences as to why you are making them a boundary. Go girl!

CHAPTER 8

Bait #3 – Exclusivity

Every girl longs to be claimed by a guy. No, really, it's true! We want to feel like we belong to someone else. Have you ever had a moment where your dad stood up for you, or made you feel like you were his only daughter? You felt like you belonged to him, and because of that, you felt loved, attended to and protected by him. Was there ever a time where your brother looked out for you and made sure that no one else harmed you or tried to do something inappropriate to you? You loved the feeling of someone saying, "Naw, she's with me, homeboy. That's MY daughter or that's MY sister, etc." For a guy to claim me, whether it be my brother looking out for me to protect me, or a husband making it known that I'm his, is a wonderful feeling. It makes me feel wanted, loved and protected as well as many other feelings.

A boyfriend pulls on this healthy desire which makes exclusivity the perfect bait to draw you into the girlfriend trap. Within the relationship, the first thing you guys establish is titles. I am now your girlfriend, and you are my boyfriend, basically saying that no one else can have you and vice versa.

You instantly feel like you have someone you can call your own that no one else can have. It's what that little girl in you has always wanted because she was starved of that feeling growing up when there were no healthy men around to see her, love her and protect her. She has always wanted a man to claim her and now she finally has it. The only thing is, a boyfriend's claim on you is not a real or legally functioning claim. When a father says you are his, that's because you really are his, either by the bloodline or legally speaking.

Exclusivity simply means to have access to someone or something for yourself while excluding all others from the same access you have. But this is just not the case for a boyfriend-girlfriend relationship. What this bait is doing is setting you up for a lie. You think you guys are exclusive, which in your mind makes you believe that you guys are in a committed relationship, but you're really not. What you really desire is commitment, and this just ain't it. What this is, is false commitment.

What Is Commitment?

We all dream of or maybe have thought about being in a committed relationship one day and growing old with someone. That is a wonderful and right desire. If you have this desire, it's not a curse nor is it evil. I believe God gives us these desires because one, we are made in his image, and he is a God who specializes in long-lasting, committed relationships. Second, so that we can mate, fill this beautiful earth with offspring and make it look more like heaven. But if you are desiring to be in a relationship or even have children with a man, then you need to understand that you are created to be committed to… first. You are created to be honored, to be lifted up high, the only one and the number one in a man's life.

> **#TheGirlfriendTrap**
>
> *You are created to be committed to.*
>
> **#TheGirlfriendTrap**

Think about this next statement: A guy can have many girlfriends, but only one wife. Literally, a guy can have 15 girlfriends in one month, but only one wife. Why is that so? This is because girlfriends are not true commitment.

Now, I know what I just said may seem odd or even offensive, depending on your culture, or what you were taught. In today's world, many people live by different rules and laws but there is no law that is greater than God's law. He revealed his law to us through His written word, and the truth is, God's intention is for a man to be with one woman and a woman to be with one man. Check it out.

"That is why a man leaves his father and mother and is united to his wife, and they become one flesh" – **Genesis 2:24 (NIV)**

Note here that the scripture says wife, not wives.

> *"He answered, 'Have you not read that he who created them from the beginning made them male and female, and said, 'Therefore a man shall leave his father and his mother and hold fast to his wife, and the two shall become one flesh?' So they are no longer two but one flesh. What therefore God has joined together, let not man separate.'"* – **Matthew 19:4-6 (ESV)**

Make another note that the scripture says the two become one, not three, four or five become one.

Let's break down the word commit using the Online Etymology Dictionary.

Co means *together* or *unite*

Mit comes from the word **mittere** which means *to send out or go out on a mission*

When you combine these 2 meanings, commitment literally means *to go or be sent out on a mission together.* When two people in a romantic relationship commit to one another, that means they entrust their entire life to one another and accept the mission God has for them to do together on this earth as one indivisible unit.

#TheGirlfriendTrap

A commitment is always sealed with a vow.

#TheGirlfriendTrap

Here's one thing to remember as long as you live: When it comes to romantic relationships, a commitment is always sealed with a vow. Let me say this one more time for the culture: A commitment is always sealed with a vow.

A **vow** is a promise made with legal and or moral enforcement. Merriam-Webster's dictionary defines it as a solemn (serious, sincere, sober, honest) promise or assertion; specifically, one by which a person is bound (held within limits) to an act, service, or condition.

This is not your, "I love you baby; I will never leave you," or "I'm yours girl; I ain't talking to nobody else but you," type situation. Vows are much deeper than some lip service in the heat of the moment, and just because you are living like you are committed to a person does not mean that you actually are.

A Bad Business Deal

True vows make commitments that are legally binding, meaning you have documentation, and it can hold up in court. It literally becomes its own entity. For example, businesses and major corporations understand what commitment is. If you apply for a loan, try to buy a car, or rent an apartment, what do you do? You sit across the table from someone and you sign a contract.

This is a legal document, stating that each party is going to commit to hold up their end of the deal.

"I'm going to give you this car. I'm going to service this car as long as you have this car." Your end of the deal may be, "I'm going to pay for this car. I'm going to hold myself accountable to paying this certain amount of money every month to have this car."

This signed document is proof of that commitment and acts as a safeguard for both parties involved. This means that if anything were to happen, if either party did not hold up their end of the deal, one has the right to pursue repayment and can take the other party to court to obtain what's legally theirs. This prevents either side from being ripped off and left hanging.

If businesses and corporations understand this about material things, if they know how to protect their own investments in this way, then why don't we protect our investments as young women? Why don't we protect the most costly, the most precious, the most fragile possession we own, our heart? Instead, we allow guys to get the best of us for the minimal cost, actually at no cost at all, or shall I say at no commitment at all. We give them all of us with no guarantee that we will get anything in return and with no insurance and protection in case of damage. **This, queen, has got to be the worst business deal ever made.** Yet, ladies all around the globe are making this kind of deal by the millions every single day.

I can't say this enough: Above all material things, cars, houses, clothes, shoes, I mean some of the most high-priced things in this world that can cost millions and millions of dollars, your heart is more valuable than all of it put together. Now, I'm not talking about that beating muscle in your chest, but I'm talking about the command center of your being, the place where your desires are, the place where your emotions live, the place where you think and make all your decisions. It is the most precious and valuable thing any human being possesses. But if you don't know its value and its desperate need to be protected, you'll treat it like trash, and you will allow other people to treat it like trash as well.

In the book of Proverbs chapter 4 verse 23, the author, inspired by God in Heaven, writes, *"Above all else, guard your heart, for everything you do flows from it.*

It's not by accident that God tells us as His precious daughters to guard our hearts above all things. This is because our heart affects everything that we do, and I mean everything. Its condition determines how and where we live, what we see as truth, how we interact with others, what we pursue in school, our self-worth...and the list goes on and on. If your heart is healthy and whole, then so are your days, but if it's shattered and broken, then nothing makes sense anymore. Your view becomes distorted, and your thoughts and decisions can no longer be trusted. It's bleeding, losing oxygen and in desperate need of spiritual aid.

#TheGirlfriendTrap

Commitment is a safeguard for your heart.

#TheGirlfriendTrap

Commitment is a safeguard for your heart. It is the only relationship where your heart can be free and thrive. It doesn't change like the style of clothing or the latest dance moves that come out every year. You won't have to worry about him leaving you with responsibility meant for 2 or be concerned about if you will still be loved in 1, 10, and even 30 years. Commitment nurtures acceptance of change in the body, mind and spirit. It allows room for failure, retries and refinement. It is the fertilizer for authentic, selfless love, a love that needs time to develop and commitment guarantees time.

So, if you know that you are created to be committed to and that commitment is always sealed with a vow, that leaves us to the only romantic relationship left between a man and a woman, marriage. Oh, how beautiful it is!

Heart Abortion

When your love or the desire to give has been awakened in you, commitment is the only thing that can contain such intense and powerful emotions and desires. Those feelings were never meant to be awakened only to be cut off later.

Women are divine givers. No really, it's in our genetic coding as we are the gender that can receive a small seed and give the world its greatest treasure, humans. I am not in the slightest way being sexist here. I totally understand that men have the ability to give to this world in great ways and do certain things much better than women. I am simply recognizing the beautiful things that women often excel in.

Our function is to help and our specialty is expansion. We have a tendency to take something small and make it grow. When we are given something in its rawest, simplest form, we have the ability to grow it and turn it into the most beautiful thing the eye has ever seen.

For example, we often are the ones to take raw foods and turn them into edible delicacies that nourish the body to thrive another day. If you give us an empty room, we will turn it into a place of comfort, filling it with DIY projects, comfy chairs, and smell goods that makes you want to stay forever. We turn houses into homes, a refuge that you can run to for shelter and safety. We turn small businesses into corporations and the list goes on and on. Whatever seed that is planted inside of us, we have the capability of growing it into something much bigger and of greater value.

So, when a seed is planted in us, by default, we prepare for growth and expansion. In fact, we jump in heart first, as we develop a posture of joyful expectation.

Think of a man planting his seed inside a woman's womb. She is now pregnant, full of joy and hopeful for tomorrow as she prepares for a beautiful child to be born. Her heart dances as she daydreams about holding her baby soon. She knows that there is no trickery going on, that the baby is surely coming as she feels her stomach grow with each rising of the sun. But after some time, the same guy that planted the seed abruptly causes trauma, ending the life that was once growing inside of her.

Whoa! Now, I know you were not expecting that. Let's be honest. What I just said was awful and downright gruesome depending on which way your imagination just took you. But it takes a serious analogy for us to understand what happens when we allow a guy into our hearts and behave in ways that permanently affect us with no commitment. He awakens our desire to give with no plans of staying to reciprocate the action. Our hearts are as precious and fragile as that growing baby in the womb.

#TheGirlfriendTrap

Your boyfriend is not committed to you.

#TheGirlfriendTrap

When a man plants a seed of expectancy there, we begin to prepare for "forever," our feelings begin to grow, and we even daydream about the future with him as we fall deeper and deeper in desire. In the midst of preparing for this relationship to last, our hearts are ripped open, ending all hope of something more to come. We are then left to mourn the loss of what was. This is the broken heart that millions of young girls and women experience on a daily basis.

Your boyfriend is not committed to you. So, if he wants to, he can have you, dump you, and go get another girl, just like that. When it's over, how can you tell your heart the same? Is there an undo button? Is there an automatic off switch that you can flip and immediately stop all the feelings and memories? Oh, how I wish there was, but there isn't.

On Purpose

God created you on purpose, with purpose and strategically planned out all of your days on this earth. When God brings a man and a woman together, it is for a divine purpose. He is too strategic to haphazardly put people together only for them to break up after some time. And because of purpose, the only relationship, romantic-wise, that He honors between a man and a woman, is marriage, because that's the only kind of relationship that has a foundation that He can build His kingdom upon.

When you create anything less than commitment, confusion is inevitable.

Let's be honest. No one knows what to do with each other as boyfriends and girlfriends. You put your precious and priceless heart in your own hands and play a horrible game of chance with it. When you create anything less than commitment, confusion is inevitable.

"Do I have sex with you or do I not? Do we move in together or do we not? Do we go on this trip together or do we not? It's not really a commitment, but it's kind of like a commitment because, you know, I am your girlfriend, you're my boyfriend," yada yada yada.

If you can walk away anytime you want to, then it's not true commitment.

But that's where we get it messed up and confused. You're not really eachothers at all. If you can walk away anytime you want to, then it's not true commitment.

What ends up happening is you make committed-like decisions in these temporary situations, like having sex, getting loans and bank accounts together, moving in together, getting tatted and more. And when it does end (most of these relationships do), you're left with the consequences of these decisions to deal with on your own. You're now emotionally and financially stuck with this person whom you're not with anymore, and who has moved on to the next girl with no hesitation. Your feelings are hurt and broken because you thought he was the only one for you, that you could never love someone, or he could never love someone more than he loved you. Girl, I know this song so well.

The best thing to do now is to rehearse the truth: "I'm not something to be toyed with, to be had and then thrown away. I'm a Queen and I am worth commitment, nothing less."

Girlfriend Confession #3

As a girlfriend, I never required anything from my boyfriend. I just assumed, like most of this dating culture does, that when you claim someone as your own and make it "official" then that's it. You guys are together. I wasn't talking to anyone else and neither was he, and so in my mind, that meant we were committed to each other. Clearly, I had no idea of what commitment really was.

I remember breaking up after some years and feeling so angry at how easy it was for him to walk away.

"Like, for real? After all these years we spent together you're just going to….leave?"

I broke up with him multiple times, times that he obliged to, but somehow I always found myself going back because I was so emotionally attached to him (which was a negative soultie created through sex). By this time, I was fighting for my health because it was such a toxic relationship emotionally. I knew it was ending, but I wasn't ready for the pain that was about to hit me head-on. When it finally ended, it ended for good! I would call periodically as a reflex to relieve the hurt I felt, but he never called me in the same way.

"Did you not care? Did you even love me?"

Those were always my thoughts. But as I began to heal and sober up with wisdom, I realized what had happened. It was so easy for him to walk away because he didn't invest much to have me. And when you don't invest anything, you don't lose anything.

*** **Do you have a girlfriend story/confession that you want to share? I would LOVE to hear it. Text me your age and confession at 708-580-8823**

How to Let Go of the Bait: Separate Temporary from Permanent

Let go of this bait of exclusivity, which is really FALSE commitment, and prepare for the real thing. In letting go of this bait, you have to know what signifies true commitment and know the difference between temporary and permanent. Boyfriend-girlfriend relationships, even dating relationships, are temporary and are not permanent like marriages are, and there are just some permanent or committed-like things that should not be done in temporary situations.

I want you to write out actions that have temporary consequences and actions that have permanent consequences when it comes to relationships.

That way, when these actions come up, you can decide if it's okay to do them based on the relationship status that you have. And queen, there are only 2 kinds of relationship statuses, single (temporary relationships) or married (a permanent relationship). If you are not married, then you are legally single, no in-between.

Help yourself preserve your own heart. To get started, use my example on the next page.

***Healthy tip: Reserve the permanent actions for a permanent relationship. Marriage!

Temporary – lasting only a short time
Permanent – to remain without an end

Temporary	VS.	Permanent
Talking on the phone		Sharing a naked picture
Changing my clothes, nail color, hairstyle		Getting a Tattoo
		Sex (the effects)

CHAPTER 9

What the Trap Creates # 1 – False Ownership

What would you do if someone took something from you that was so valuable, so dear to you, and made it their own? What would you do if your boyfriend took something from you and did that? Or better yet, took "you" and did that?

We all know what ownership is. Everyone owns something, whether you own a pair of pants, some shoes, or maybe a phone. Yeah, let's stick with the last example. Say for instance you own an iPhone, and you know iPhones cost a lot of money. You allow your friend to borrow it to make a phone call. But what if they took it and then put their own lock code in it, or their own fingerprint in it? What if they took your case off and put theirs on it? They even erased your contacts and put their own contacts in. How would you feel about that? Giirrrl listen, you don't even have to tell me how you would feel, because if you're anything like me, you would be too upset!

"How are you going to take something that's not yours, and make it your own? You didn't buy that phone, I did. You don't pay the bill on that every month, I do!"

Hmm. You don't like it when someone takes something of yours and makes it their own, right? So, why do you allow guys to do that to you?

One of the reasons why I will never be a girlfriend again is because becoming "his girl" gives him a false sense of ownership of me. This is why once you allow a guy to feel he owns you, he will always feel he has a right to what's his.

Now, I don't mean own you in a bad way,

"I own you! Shut up, girl, and do what I tell you to do." Naw!

What I'm saying is, he literally thinks you are his. In his mind, he thinks, "my girlfriend, my woman, nobody else can have her but me." So, guess what? If you are his, then he feels he can do whatever he wants with you. He may feel he has the right to touch you anywhere on your body and kiss you, to come see you whenever he wants to, have sex with you and so much more.

This is an error all the way through, simply because you are not his girl no matter what is said out of the mouth. By allowing a guy to think that you are his is cheapening yourself big time because he did absolutely nothing to have you. As we discussed before, a woman remains under the covering and authority of her father, and she continues to carry his last name to show who she belongs to. If a guy has not yet given you his last name then guess what? You don't belong to him.

#TheGirlfriendTrap

If a guy has not yet given you his last name, then you don't belong to him.

#TheGirlfriendTrap

If you are not his, then why would you allow him to believe you are? That is false behavior and it's very misleading. He has not invested anything of value. He has not done any hard work to have you. He has not committed to you and until that happens, he can't claim any ownership where there is none. Period!

One of the reasons why girls feel so cheated when the relationship ends is because she gave herself to him thinking that she was his to have. She in return invests in him, making him look better, feel better, doing things for him that only a wife should do for her husband. And when it ends, she feels as if all her hard work went down the drain. That's because it did!

Set Your Price

Think back on that original masterpiece as it is covered and protected, sitting in the highest place in the building. Because it is so special, because it is of a high value, whoever wants it for themselves will have to pay the high dollar amount to have it. Period! They're not about to give it away for free or even for a discounted price. No one will be able to even say they own it until they paid for it.

Let me use myself as an example. God created me full of beauty and in His image. I am His very own masterpiece, and if any guy would like to have me as his own, then he is going to have to pay the price to have me. He has to take the necessary steps to be able to claim this masterpiece as his own and experience all the goodness that comes with it. He's going to have to commit to me because commitment is the only real "ownership" there is when it comes to relationships. You must start thinking of yourself in this way.

Okay, queen, I get it. I totally understand our culture and how we like to claim people so no one else can have them, but that's just it. Someone else can have them if they wanted to, which proves the point that they are not yours to begin with and vice versa. This part of our girl chat may be stirring up feelings of disappointment and even panic. I have a feeling that these thoughts may be trying to creep into your mind.

"But he is mine and I am his! If I don't say he is mine, then how will other girls know to back off? What if I'm never chosen again? What if there is no guy who will claim me as his own again? If I don't let him claim me, then he will leave me"

I know the desperate plea.

"Wait, don't go! I am willing to be claimed at a discounted value if you will just make me feel wanted, even if it's for a short time."

To not claim a guy as yours or let him claim you as his girl in today's culture is unheard of and outright terrifying. Because women feel they will "lose their man" if they don't...comply. But can I say something that may offend you (change your normal way of thinking)? Only women who don't know their value feel that they will lose a guy. Women who are confident in themselves and sure of what God has invested in them know that they are the prize at ALL times. They know that they bring value to a guy's life, and it's the guy who would be losing out, not her. (Pause for a second and let that sink in.)

This is why the first bait deals with the idea of value. It's soooooooo important for you to establish your value and know it without a shadow of a doubt because without that knowledge, you will always discredit and discount yourself. Our culture of dating trains you to settle for less, and if all women are settling, then you will feel pressured to do the same out of fear that no guy would want to be with you. Giiirrrl, it's a trick from the pit of hell.

Yes, there are guys who will not want to be with you, but it's not because your standards are too high. It's because their standards are too low. They are so used to not having to do much to get a girl, and because of that, they are not willing to rise to your standards, really any standards at all. That's his issue, not yours. And if you think about it, why would you want to be connected to a guy like that? He is showing you his work ethic in life.

When things get too hard, he chooses not to work harder to get it. Instead, he taps out and settles for what's readily available. Is that the kind of guy you want to be your covering, lead your home and father your children? If so, then once you let him have you, that will be the peak of you all's life together because more than likely, he won't be looking to pursue anything greater with you. Trust me when I say this. I see it happening right before my eyes in the lives of women around me.

In order to go from an uncovered woman, a woman unsubmitted to her father (God), to a covered woman, a woman who surrenders her heart in full submission to her father (God), you are going to have to position yourself differently. It may come across as strange and different, but it will be one of the best moves you ever make for your self-esteem and your life in general.

But let me be the first to tell you this or be an enforcement to what you have already heard: Your value is NEVER based on a man choosing you or wanting to be with you. You are valuable all by yourself! That alone should boost your confidence to another level. There are things in you that a man needs, and the right one will realize his deficiency and come asking you to credit his life. YES, you!

So don't you, for another second, think that you are not worth the wait or investment. You are the prize at ALL times, ALL times, ALL times, and prizes don't devalue themselves to get in the reach of a mediocre contestant. No! She waits for the right one to present himself, and because he has enough heart and endurance, because he fulfilled the set price to have you, only then does it make him the winner.

So, masterpiece, now is your chance. Now is the time to make it known to yourself and the rest of the world just how expensive you really are. With all the valuable qualities that you possess, what price are you going to set it at? Let me help you... $Commitment.00. Now, doesn't that feel good?

It's a Privilege

It took many failures to finally succeed in knowing the truth about myself, and because I'm so valuable, because I am this masterpiece, the truth is that it

is a privilege to have me. It is a privilege to have my attention. It is a privilege to call me on the phone. It is a privilege to know my thoughts, desires and dreams. It is a privilege to spend time with me. It is a privilege to taste my lips and even see my body, let alone touch it. This is not arrogance or being uppity and bougie. It's confidence! When you become aware of your value, you will begin to act like the royalty that you are. You will start to look at yourself in a totally different light. You'll start to dress a different way. You'll start to change the friends that you have and change the company that you allow to entertain you, all because you are certain of who you are and what you possess. Say it with me and get used to it, "It is a privilege to be with me."

I don't know if you are at this place like I was, tired of allowing a guy to drag your heart through the mud because you are giving yourself to him without him sacrificing anything to have you and not requiring him to acknowledge your true value. But if you are, that internal conflict that you are wrestling with will not go away. It will only get louder if you don't confront it head-on.

Queen, hold your head up high. It's never too late to assume your high position in the gallery. When God told me my worth, I didn't waste another day on the discounted shelf. I set my price, and let me tell you, I'm far from cheap, baby. I don't worry about missing out on any guy because I know the right guy, God's guy, will have enough to pay for me.

Take this same confidence and hold on to it. You're going to need it as you make that climb to the top shelf. Come on up. It's spacious up here.

Girlfriend Confession # 4

I let him have me for free. As I made myself so easily available, it became obvious that he was getting used to it. I made things so easy for him that he got comfortable with no urgency to get his own stuff in order or move forward in life. I found myself always pushing him to do things that a man should already be moving toward accomplishing. A woman is never meant to carry a man, and I was doing it, and worn out as I did.

He would start to get upset when I wouldn't do things that he should have had to work for and thus getting something he did not deserve. I had a car, he didn't. So, I was the one always driving. That statement alone runs deep. I always felt I was settling and that feeling increased as time went on, but when he would start to get mad because I wouldn't use my own car to pick him up and take him places, I knew I had messed up big time. It would lead to arguments that only showed the symptoms of the issue at hand. I would then struggle with feeling bad for not giving him what was technically mine and not his.

Ladies, I know I am not the only one who has struggled with male pleasing, feeling pressured to give a guy something that he has no rights to. I would give in, as he manipulated me to believe I was wrong or that I didn't care about him if I didn't do it. But I now know something that I will never forget as long as I live: **I don't owe a guy anything!!** My body is not his and neither are my possessions. I will never again succumb to the pressure to give up what's mine to keep. Until he has committed to me, I am not his, and I won't for a second allow him to believe that I am.

*** Do you have a girlfriend story/confession that you want to share? I would LOVE to hear it. Text me your age and confession at 708-580-8823

Key# 1: Take Back What's Yours!

A privilege is an advantage granted to a person that puts them in a better position than where they were before. Girl, your whole life is an advancement, and it's time that you see it for yourself. Unlock the trap by writing out some privileges that a guy will gain once he commits to you and see for yourself why you can't afford to give yourself to him before that commitment takes place. These privileges are yours to take back from a guy you have given them to so that you can keep and protect them for the committed one (husband).

This is going to help you see your value in a greater light and boost your confidence as you climb to the top shelf. Use my list as a guide to get started.

It is a privilege to:

1. Talk to me on the phone at any time of the day and see into my mind
2. Engage with those I hold dear to me (my trusted circle)
3. Hold my body
4. Kiss me
5. Spend alone time with me
6. Have sex with me
7. Have me cook for you
8. Have me clean for you
9. Have me wash your clothes
10. Have me Iron your clothes
11. Have me encourage you and build you up
12. Have me organize your living space (closet, drawers, room, etc.)
13. Have me do your hair
14. Have me manicure your nails
15. Have me give you massages
16. To know my deepest desires and secrets
17. Have me help to raise your kids and teach them godly principles
18. Have me help your business grow
19. Enjoy my creativity
20. Have me take care of you when you're sick
21. Have my opinion when you need to make difficult decisions, solve difficult problems, or avoid mistakes
22. Have me defend you against criticism
23. Have me encourage your good qualities (bring out your best)
24. Have me discourage your bad qualities (avoid your worst)
25. Have me add to your financial security in retirement
26. Have me support you when you are in school or out of work
27. Have me to share life's important events with (our children's births, marriages, etc.)
28. Have me to get you through difficult times (deaths of friends and family)

It is a privilege to:

Okay! Now it's your turn.

CHAPTER 10
What the Trap Creates #2 – No Chase

When a man thinks that he owns you, he thinks that he has ownership rights, which leads to this reason of why you should break free from this girlfriend trap, because it automatically turns down the chase. Girl, this is huge.

In today's culture, you see a lot of women chasing men. Pause! Let's have a moment of silence for all the women who have lost their minds. I'm not even going to act like I understand and agree because I don't. It's so backward, and I believe it's like this because we don't know who we are. We don't know our purpose as women, and we don't know that we were created to be pursued, like a rare jewel hidden in the deep.

There's a popular truth that you may have heard before, "he who finds a wife finds a good thing, and he obtains favor in the sight of God" (Proverbs 18:22). The keywords are, "he who finds."

Another word for find is "obtain," but follow me here.

When God created man, He created a hunter, a worker, a master builder and cultivator. He created man to take something in its infant stage and help it grow, bringing the beauty out of it and giving it identity as it grows, like a gardener. He didn't just create man to build materially, but he also created him to build emotionally and spiritually. He created a man to build a family which includes pursuing a woman and making her a wife.

No Time to Waste

If a guy feels that he already has you as his own, then he will no longer be motivated to pursue you. This is one of the biggest reasons why I say I will never be a girlfriend again. As a girlfriend, not only did I make myself so available and make him feel like he already had me, but that was it. I stayed in a relationship for four years too long and four years that I can never get back.

Now, you may be thinking, "Oh my goodness, four years. That's real love. Y'all were in it to win it. That's what I call relationship goals." Think again, my queen!

#TheGirlfriendTrap

To be some guy's long-term girlfriend is not a compliment to you but an insult.

#TheGirlfriendTrap

To be some guy's long-term girlfriend is not a compliment to you but an insult. He has no purpose with you, and when you don't know what to do with something, you waste time with it, taking advantage of it, even mistreating and abusing it.

Both of you have divine callings to be a part of God's kingdom building on this earth. This includes showing the world the value of commitment, how to love each other, how to steward money, how to be fruitful in deeds and multiply, how to raise whole human beings to glorify the God who created them and so much more. All this can only be done on this side of heaven, within the age of time, and time can never be had again.

Your time is precious, and you don't have a lot of it. Never let a guy who does not know what he wants and who has yet to get his life instructions from the Lord, pursue you. Maturity builds manhood, and when a young man has vision and purpose, he quickly knows if a woman is someone he wants to marry.

He will waste no time ushering her into her calling as his wife because he is a man of action and he recognizes the urgency of time and purpose. Why would he play around and string her heart along, potentially allowing another guy to come in and swoop her up? To a man who lives on purpose, that is straight foolishness to him.

Just a Convenience

Some guys will hold on to you for selfish pleasures, so you can temporarily fulfill his emotional and sexual needs. That is until another girl comes along who can do it much better than you. So, truthfully speaking, you are not his girlfriend, you are a convenience to him and just another option to pick from.

This is what we have to understand. When a guy doesn't know his purpose, when he has failed to receive his life instructions from the Lord, you will find him doing anything of convenience, anything that satisfies his immediate desires at that time. And when he doesn't have instructions on what to do, what he will end up doing is...doing you! The only way to stop yourself from being a guy's "convenience" is to free yourself from living a convenient life.

You have to be intentional with your moves. You have to get clarity on where you are going and how you are going to get there. Once you do that, you eliminate all people and relationships who are literally wasting your gifts and time. Think about it; why would you invest your heart and time into a guy who really doesn't know if he wants to be with you? There is only one logical answer: When you don't know your purpose in life, you will allow a guy to have no purpose with you as well.

> 66 #TheGirlfriendTrap
>
> *When you don't know your purpose in life, you will allow a guy to have no purpose with you.*
>
> #TheGirlfriendTrap 99

The reason why so many girls stay girlfriends is because they don't require a guy to work for them. Think about it; he already gets your body any time he wants it; he tells everyone else that you are his and to back off; he has the house with you, the bank account and even kids with you. He already has full access to you with no commitment at all. Why would he buy something he gets for free? I know I wouldn't.

Why would he feel he needs to do anything else special or above the ordinary? That just goes to show you that he doesn't know your value, and you are not requiring him to know it. Now, don't get me wrong here; he is perfectly fine, peachy cool might I add, to not put in work if you were an ordinary chick. But you are not ordinary. You are extraordinary. A masterpiece! You can't be had out of convenience.

Make Him Work

When you don't require a man to work for you, it's disrespectful to yourself, and it's also disrespectful to him because you're crippling him. God has put so much inside of a man and the capabilities to go after what he wants, including a woman. When you lower the bar, you stifle his growth, preventing him from rising up to the man that he's destined to be. It's like tying a grown man's shoes when he is more than capable of doing it himself.

Now that you know it is a privilege to be with you, your standards should shoot through the roof.

#TheGirlfriendTrap

Having standards eliminates all the guys who can't rise up to those standards.

#TheGirlfriendTrap

A standard is something that is acceptable. It is a measurement by which another person is compared to. Standards are those things that if another person does not measure up to it, then it's a hard no for allowing them to have a relationship with you. I like to think of standards as those things that are non-negotiable, and they are needed for the health and advancement of my life or the life of the relationship.

Having standards eliminates all the guys who can't rise up to those standards, or who are not willing to rise up to those standards. This makes room for the very one whom you are created for and is created for you. He's the one who's going to see your value, so much so, that he will want to do whatever it takes to have you.

You were meant to be pursued, as if someone were searching for a rare jewel that can only be found in the deep. But when that rare jewel rises to the surface, it begins to erode and blend in with the rest of the dull rocks, taking away the excitement of the chase. We see the value of things more clearly when we have to put in hard work to get it and being convenient simply takes away the hard work. Allow him the satisfaction of working hard for what he wants. This will cause him to see your value more clearly.

This means it's time to get out of arm's reach. Any guy that wants you should face a challenge to have you. Trust me, he wants to be challenged. He wants to feel as if he is getting an exclusive deal, something no other man has.

Hide yourself deep within purpose and within God's word, so that the only way to reach you is if he is moving in purpose himself and is in God's face. If he is close enough, God will whisper in his ear exactly where you are, giving him the green light to pursue you. Queen, this is the beauty of having a relationship with God. When you allow him to cover you, He will protect you. He will protect you from predators, guys who only come to crush the beauty out of you and will only allow the one in that will strive to love you like He loves you.

Girlfriend Confession #5

"When are we going to get married?"

I was either asking this question or thinking about it. Either way, it was always on my mind. As a believer, I knew that when you got into a relationship, marriage was to follow...eventually. What I didn't know was that in order to get married, you have to be ready to marry.

Here we are, both in our early twenties and as immature as can be. I was in no way ready to take on such a life-changing commitment such as marriage and neither was he. That didn't stop us from getting into a relationship. But it should have! 1 year goes by, then 2, then 3, then...wait, what are we even doing?

Why am I still a girlfriend after all this time? I was tormented internally. I felt the divine desires swell up inside me to give to him, help him and expand his life, and I desperately wanted to do all those things with total freedom but I couldn't. I constantly sensed God telling me no, to stop and get out of the relationship, that it wasn't the right relationship nor was it the proper time to do all those things.

I desired commitment but I was caught up in convenience. Don't even get me started on the desire for sex. By this time, I was learning more about respecting sex and God who created it and being in a relationship where I could not fully express myself in that way with peace and joy was torture.

There was absolutely no purpose and thus no advancement. Had I not pursued God and hounded him on why I was created, I believe I would have still been a girlfriend, crying the same tune and wasting time like so many queens are doing right now. I for sure wouldn't be writing this book, and I would have still been preventing the very things that God put in me to come out. The pursuit of purpose saved my life. Seriously!

*** **Do you have a girlfriend story/confession that you want to share? I would LOVE to hear it. Text me your age and confession at 708-580-8823**

Key #2: Set the Standard and Keep It

If a guy wants you, make him pursue you!

Unlock the trap by writing out a list of standards that a guy has to **do** or **be** in order to have you as his own. Make sure they are foundational things that must be there and not surface or selfish things like skin color. This will give you clarity on what you are and are not willing to stand for. I started my own list. Feel free to use it as a guide.

***Healthy Tip: Knowing the purpose that God specifically assigned to your life will help you create this list and ultimately help you choose who is suited for you as a future spouse. This takes time as you grow in your relationship with Him, so feel free to come back and visit this list as you learn more about yourself. Every person has a reason for living and that includes loving, tending to the homeless and needs of others and praying for people. That alone gives you plenty to do each day.

When it comes to this list, there are some things that all women are created to have, one being respect. Start there but don't end there.

P.S. "Respect is just a minimum" – Lauryn Hill

These Are My Standards (What's acceptable)

1. He has to believe in Jesus and bear fruit of the Holy Spirit.
2. He has to have a job.
3. He has to be financially responsible
4. He has to have his own transportation and place to live separate from me (showing an ability to take care of self)
5. He has to live a life of integrity and honesty
6. He has to be a protector (of his own heart and others)
7. He has to talk to men in my family, which shows honor to me and his willingness to be held accountable
8. He has to respect me (chivalry)
9. He has to respect my boundaries (and have some of his own)
10. He has to respect sex (& honor God with his body)
11. He has to respect his own body (free of drugs, abuse, etc.)
12. He has to be fathering his children if he has any
13. He has to respect his parents

Okay! Now it's your turn.

Feel free to write out the opposite of each standard so that you can clearly see what you are NOT willing to accept.

What's Acceptable	VS.	What's NOT Acceptable

CHAPTER 11

What the Trap Creates #3 – False Expectations

How many of us have expected someone to do something for us and was so disappointed when they didn't do it. If you could see me right now, then you would see that I have both hands in the air. For example, when my friend would tell me that she was going to go out with me and then flake on me at the last minute, it sucked! But let's be honest, how many of us have been one of those people to say that we were going to do something and then bail out at the last minute?

It's natural to have expectations in all different kinds of relationships, like with your parents, your friends, and even your teachers. Expectations are good and healthy, and we are supposed to have them. I'd say, if you don't have expectations of any kind, then that's a little scary. I would have to question if you are even a human.

The definition of expectation is believing that something will happen or should happen. Let's stick with "should happen." If you go to a movie theater and you buy tickets, you expect a movie to play on that big screen when you sit down. If you go through a fast food drive-through line and pay your money, you expect food to be delivered to you with no delay. If you paid money to go to school, college students, then you expect a teacher to be there to teach you what you're supposed to learn. Expectations, we all have them. But not all expectations are right expectations, and sometimes, we put expectations in the wrong places and with the wrong people.

My Everything

When I was a girlfriend, I had so many high expectations of him. I expected him to pick up that phone every time I called him. I expected him to be sensitive to all my feelings and emotions. I expected him to love me like no one else has ever loved me before. I expected him to know what I was thinking. I expected him to make me happy and to heal my broken heart. I even expected him to give me validation. I expected so much from this boyfriend, but the keyword is "boyfriend." I expected him to do things that he didn't have the skill to do nor the obligation to do. Boyfriends don't have the skill nor obligation to fulfill your expectations.

There were a lot of things that I was expecting from a boyfriend that could only be fulfilled by a father. If you're like me, you grew up without a consistent, present love of a father. I didn't know what it felt like to have that male companionship. I didn't know what it felt like to be fully loved by a man. So I go and get a boyfriend, and because I'm human, I expected him to automatically fill all my voids, to fill my heart up with everything I'd been missing.

> **66** #TheGirlfriendTrap
>
> ***Boyfriends don't have the skill nor obligation to fulfill your expectations.***
>
> #TheGirlfriendTrap **99**

But reality is, boyfriends are not fathers. They can never replace a father's love, direction and validation. That was a false expectation I was putting on him and like a true boyfriend, he failed. He did not have the skills to fulfill that expectation.

You get into a relationship with a guy and you expect him to be everything to you, to be the world to you. Well, first off, that is too high of an expectation to put not just on a boyfriend but on any human being. And second, he didn't create you. You were created by one God up above and your heart is designed to be completely fulfilled by Him. There is a gaping void within your being that can only be filled by God and until you realize that, you will forever be searching. You will search for love, high and mostly low, year after year, trying to get a man to do something that he can't.

Don't Leave Me

Let's get right down to it. When I had sex with him, giving him my most private possession, I would expect him to cherish me. I would expect him to respect me, to be faithful to me because I was thinking, "Hey, I'm faithful to you. I'm giving you all of me."

I expected him to hold me up in the highest position in his life and to love me forever and never leave me. Pay attention to what I just said, "love me forever and never leave me." Ha! What a naive and flat-out false expectation I placed on him, simply because he was my boyfriend.

He didn't have an obligation to me. He was not my husband! So, if I gave him my body, and he said, "thank you, deuces," then guess what? He can do that because he was not committed to me.

Say for instance you're thinking about or you are living with your boyfriend right now. What are you expecting from him? Are you expecting him to stay with you? Are you expecting him to pay the bills, to clean up and to do all these things that you think a man should? Y'all could be living in an apartment together right now and he could say, "You know what, I'm done with you. I don't like you anymore; the booty is old. Peace!"

This leaves you with the bills to pay, with all these responsibilities that just fell upon you, maybe even leaving you homeless. Now you have to hurry up and find a friend to live with or go back home. Where is the peace, safety, comfort and stability in a life like that? There is none!

No woman should ever have to worry if a man will still be with her the next day or even year. When you are in a committed marriage, you won't have to worry about that. You won't have to worry about being a single mother, or who is going to help pay the bills. You won't have to worry about your heart being abandoned, left alone to pick up the broken pieces.

If you pay $10 worth of a gift, wouldn't it be silly of you to expect a $100 value in return? If I buy something cheap, I'm going to expect it to be what it is, cheap. So if it breaks in a couple of weeks or months, more than likely my response would be, "oh, I knew it was going to break. It was only $10."

When you set your standards really low, don't expect him to rise above those standards. A guy will rise up to the level of standards you set because reality is, guys will only do what you allow them to do. If you allow him to treat you like some low-value, common object, then he will treat you that way. But if you raise your standards and require honor and respect for your name, body, and time, he'll treat you like the masterpiece that you really are. Expect it!

Girlfriend Confession #6

I made a god out of my boyfriend. Even though he could never fulfill those impossible expectations, it didn't stop me from pressuring him to try.

"Love me perfectly! Hold me. Comfort me. Take my stress away. Make me feel good about myself. Give me my worth. Approve of me. Stay with me...stay!"

I tightly clung to him out of fear that I would lose the male affection that I so desperately desired. If I let go of this god, who would I turn to? Who was going to replace what I was getting from him, though not much? One of the biggest reasons why I believe girls stay with guys with no commitment is because they are looking for someone to complete them, not realizing that only God can do that.

When I decided that I was going to let go of the idol I made out of my boyfriend, it was the most terrifying decision I had ever faced at that time. I knew about God, was even in a relationship with Him, but I didn't have enough faith to completely trust Him to be completely God to me without any idols.

That didn't stop God from pursuing me, and I'm so grateful that it didn't. I made a decision to walk away from what I knew deep down inside was not for me and I ran, heart shattered, into God's arms. I placed every ounce of my emotional weight upon Him, and I found Him to be strong enough to handle it. Not only did he reassure me of my worth and validation in him, but he fulfilled every expectation that I had placed in my boyfriend.

He continues to fulfill my every expectation till this very day. What I was searching for my entire life, he gave to me within 1 year of letting my boyfriend go. I now put all my expectations in Him (not perfectly but actively), and He has not failed me. He has promised to never leave me, and He promises to never leave you too. Expect Him to keep His word because He is not a liar.

"...Never will I leave you; never will I forsake you." – **God, Hebrews 13:5 (NIV)**

*** **Do you have a girlfriend story/confession that you want to share? I would LOVE to hear it. Text me your age and confession at 708-580-8823**

Key #3: Identify Your Expectations & Place Them Where They Should Go

What expectations have you put in a boyfriend? On the next page, you will find a list of expectations along with columns designated for boyfriend, husband, and God. For each expectation, write the letter "T" for true and "F" for false under each column to identify who can truly fulfill that expectation. No one is perfect in this world but ideally speaking is the approach I'm asking you to take when deciding. This is a time for honesty, so think carefully concerning each expectation.

Use this key to unlock the trap and no longer live with the disappointment of unmet expectations because you have placed them in the wrong person. From this day forward, only put expectations on people who you know can fulfill them and are willing to fulfill them. Use my example to help you get started.

P.S. feel free to add more expectations that you have noticed that you misplaced.

Expectations	Boyfriend	(Godly) Husband	(Father) God
Heal my pain	F	F	T
Never Leave me	F	T	T
Love me	F	T	T
Give me Identity	F	F	T
Pay My Bills	F	T	T
Make Me Happy			
Give me Purpose			
Give me a solution to every problem I have			
Protect me			
Live With Me			
Have Sex With Me			
Know me inside and out			

CHAPTER 12

What the Trap Creates #4 – No Rights

A right is something that is owed to you. More specifically, it is a moral or legal entitlement to act a certain way or to gain certain things in light of a specific event.

When you get into a relationship with a guy, and you are calling each other boyfriend and girlfriend, literally, the only people who recognize that connection are you and him. There is absolutely no foundation underneath it. There's no legal foundation. So, if something were to happen with this person that you're spending all your time with, investing your heart and most precious things in, maybe they got into a bad car wreck or even passed away, what rights do you have as a girlfriend?

Wife vs. Girlfriend

Unfortunately, there are men out there who cheat on their wives. Women cheat too, of course, but that's another conversation for another day. When men cheat, it is a horrible situation, but I'm going to use this as an example here. If this man who cheated dies, and he was having an affair with another woman on the side, who do you think all the legal matters will go to? The woman on the side, or the wife? You got it right: the wife.

The woman on the side is so distraught. She wants to be a part of everything that is going on with her deceased love affair. She wants to go to his funeral.

She wants to do all these privileged activities. But guess what? She has no right or entitlement to do those things. She has nothing, and if the wife declares that she can't go to the funeral, then she better not show up to the funeral.

The wife has the rights to everything her husband has, whether he is living or has transitioned to the afterlife. Even in sickness and death, she steps into the role of an agent with the power of attorney. This means that she makes all the big decisions, like deciding his fate, if he will continue to be on life support or not, or what happens to his money and assets. Everything goes to her.

Let's think about heaven for a moment. When God created man and woman in the Garden of Eden, he created them within the union of marriage. This was the first marriage ever established within humanity. Within that union, he told them to do some things. He told them to be fruitful and multiply, meaning to reproduce, to build and to fill the earth together. Not only did he give that command to man and woman, but he gave that command to husband and wife. When God created marriage, he placed privileges and rights within that union that no other relationship has access to. Marriage is entitled to privileges and rights.

When I say I'm never going to allow another guy to have me as a girlfriend, it's not because I don't like the word. It's literally because I understand my function. I understand the difference between a girlfriend and a wife, and I realize the divine status that I've been called to as a young woman. You should too. If you desire to be in a romantic relationship with a man, then the only way that God has called you to do that is within the blessings of marriage. Point-blank, period!

This is because God is the creator and representation of commitment. When you accept Jesus as Lord and savior of your life, you enter into a commitment with God, yes, a marriage. If he commits to you, never hesitating to choose you, never playing around with your heart or questioning his love for you, then it's only right that he would create a union, like marriage, to reflect his nature to use as a blueprint for you to follow.

God has shown you how you are supposed to be treated as a young woman in relation to any man who is pursuing you. He set this high standard for you, as his precious daughter, so that you will know your worth and never have to question your status or where you stand in the heart of a man. Never let a man live below the standard that your father has set for you.

By his infinite wisdom and authority, He placed certain rights and privileges within the boundaries of a committed relationship, rights and privileges that only husbands and wives have the blessing and freedom to enjoy. Any other man and woman relationship that engages in these activities outside of commitment is breaking his divine law. He created a husband and wife to:

1. Become one in body, soul and spirit.
2. Cohabitate (live with each other) and make everything they have separately to become one.
3. Enjoy the gift of sex.
4. Have children and build a family.
5. Leave a divine legacy of marital commitment, unity and of true worship to God and to tell the truth about the Gospel of Jesus.

Since we have a better understanding of God's perfect creation of marriage, answer this question. What can God do with a boyfriend and a girlfriend relationship? He can't tell them to come together and reproduce. They can't, by God's law, become one in body (sex), soul and spirit, live together, fill the earth together, build together, and there's no foundation legally nor spiritually holding them up. Boyfriends and girlfriends were never made by God; therefore, they have no access to the rights and privileges given by God within the boundaries of commitment. It's an illegal entity. When something is illegal, there is no insurance or coverage, so when things break and become damaged, and they will, it's your loss!

#TheGirlfriendTrap

Never let a man live below the standard that your father has set for you.

#TheGirlfriendTrap

Heaven Has the Final Say

Not only does a wife have rights down here on this earth, but a wife has heavenly rights. So, when things go down, when things are stolen, when the husband is not acting right or somebody tries to come in and take what's hers, she has the right to go before the throne of God with boldness and declare what's hers. She can declare that he is her husband, that her family is blessed, that this is her money, her house and her business. When she goes before the throne in prayer, God honors her request because He gave her the right to do so. She has a right before God because she made a covenant with Him and her husband, and God is going to back her up all the way.

> 66 #TheGirlfriendTrap
>
> *A girlfriend can't help a man do anything because she doesn't have any heavenly rights to do so.*
>
> #TheGirlfriendTrap 99

A girlfriend is not a helpmate. When God said that it is not good for a man to be alone, he was talking about a certain kind of man who was already in a position of purpose, and when he brought woman into the man's life to be his helper, it wasn't a random chick. It wasn't a chick that he thought was cute, who had a big booty and cute face. It was a woman that was divinely placed in his life with an order from God to help him make this world look like heaven. A girlfriend can't help a man do anything, because she doesn't have any heavenly rights to do so.

> 66 #TheGirlfriendTrap
>
> *If you're going to let a man call you anything, let him call you wife.*
>
> #TheGirlfriendTrap 99

My beautiful queen don't live below your divine status. Don't settle for anything less. You're not a girlfriend. You're not a side chick. You're not a fling. You're not a one-night stand. You're not a random. You're not a friend with benefits. You're not a placeholder or a convenience. You're not even a baby momma. Stop wearing that title with pride. You weren't called to any of these functions and when you answer to them, you short change your entire life, your purpose and your destiny. If you're going to let a man call you anything, let him call you wife.

Girlfriend Confession #7

Talk about a loss! When I broke up with my boyfriend, everything I did in that relationship and everything I gave emotionally and physically, was lost. Experiencing such a loss like that sobered me up real quick to see just how broken this dating culture truly is. After all the heartache and pain, sunshine and rain, I had nothing to show for it but the consequences of my sinful and misguided ways of thinking and acting. I got no repayments for the broken heart, the emotional floods, and soul theft. Why didn't anyone tell me about this part? What was I thinking would happen afterwards?

I wasn't ready to face the reality that it was all for nothing. When success comes along, girlfriends never get recognition. Why? Because she never made the team. All the work and time she put in to help better him as a man now goes to the next woman to enjoy! Well, that's if he miraculously has a change of heart and allows God to completely take over his life. If not, then the next girl will suffer just as much as the previous girl did or even worse. Oh, how I don't wish that on any woman.

After acknowledging that, I had to work with God to let go of the fantasy of him treating the next woman much better than how he treated me. Reality is, he should, and I had to understand that what he did after me was none of my business, because we were never supposed to be together in sin like we were anyway. Legally speaking, he was never mine and I was never his, so it made sense for me to let go of him in my heart and expect nothing back from him in repayment. Many women suffer today from never forgiving an ex because she feels like he owes her and should pay her back for how wrong he treated her. But the truth is, he doesn't owe her anything. He doesn't owe YOU anything. That's tough to hear but you have to acknowledge that you both willingly decided to sin together, and with all sin, the wages is death. That means some things are going to die because of it and most of the time, it's the relationship.

"When you were slaves of sin, you were free in regard to righteousness [you had no desire to conform to God's will]. So what benefit did you get at that time from the things of which you are now ashamed? [None!] For the outcome of those things is death! But now since you have been set free from sin and

*have become [willing] slaves to God, you have your benefit, resulting in sanctification [being made holy and set apart for God's purpose], and the outcome [of this] is eternal life. For the wages of sin is death, but the free gift of God [that is, His remarkable, overwhelming gift of grace to believers] is eternal life in Christ Jesus our Lord."- **Romans 6:20-23 (AMP)***

You have already been paid for your sufferings and hard work. It's just not in the form of a blessing like you thought it would be. Blessings never come from planting seeds in the devil's ground. That is a spiritual law and the sooner you understand that the better off you will be. If I were you (which I was), I would take my wages and leave, quickly, before something worse happens. And if you stay in those sinful conditions, something worse will happen. We all reap what we sow, and this kind of loss is what happens when we lay down with the devil.

*"Do not be deceived: God is not mocked, for whatever one sows, that will he also reap. For the one who sows to his own flesh will from the flesh reap corruption, but the one who sows to the Spirit will from the Spirit reap eternal life." - **Galatians 6:7-8 (ESV)***

When it came to me and my then boyfriend, we never had legal consent from heaven to give ourselves to each other. When I understood that, it helped me run even faster to God so that He could help me heal, and I thanked Him even more for saving me and getting me out of that illegal contract that I made with that guy and the devil. When you involve yourself in illegal activity, it's better to escape limping than to never escape at all and lose your life.

That relationship was the last time I idolized a guy and since then I have gone through many processes of healing. Now, I laugh looking back at it all and I use the lessons I learned to help other young women learn theirs.

Here is a simple one; before you put in any work in a relationship, make sure God is the focus and you are a wife first.

*** **Do you have a girlfriend story/confession that you want to share? I would LOVE to hear it. Text me your age and confession at 708-580-8823**

Key #4: Know Your Rights

Unlock the trap by making a list of what a girlfriend is entitled to and what a wife is entitled to when it comes to a relationship with a man. If you need help, just ask Google about the laws in your home state when it comes to a wife and a girlfriend and what either gets in the case of a breakup or divorce. Which side do you fall on? Is it worth it?

P.S. Giving someone all you have with no security is NEVER worth it! It is the epitome of foolishness and the unequal exchange.

Rights/Privileges

Girlfriend   VS.   Wife

Girlfriend	Wife
	Financial earnings $$$

PART 3
Your Way of Escape

CHAPTER 13
Your Way of Escape

Wow! We have talked about a lot, 12 chapters worth of good stuff on what a girlfriend is, how girls become girlfriends, the bait, what the trap creates and so much in between. We have been talking about switching out the bait for truth and keys on how to unlock the trap. But we all know that one can let go of the bait and unlock the trap door and still remain stuck inside. This is because when you are used to a certain way of doing things, you simply don't know any other way to go.

This last part of our girl talk is going to be all about how to get out of the trap and stay out for good. We are about to establish a strategy on how to approach dating and the opposite sex from here on out.

I'm sure you have many questions springing up in that beautiful heart of yours.

"If I'm not a girlfriend and I know I'm called to be a wife, what am I in between that time?"

"How do I date and what exactly does that look like?"

Okay! You're about to get all those answers and more, and I think you will be excitingly shocked when you know what they are. But before we get to that, let me just say this: I apologize to you. No seriously, I do.

I want to give you the apology that you will never get from the culture you have been raised in. I apologize for how this culture has made you feel like your value is based on a relationship status. Our dating culture is truly set up for our moral and spiritual failure and we all are a product of it. It has conditioned us to have a consumer mentality, to spend everything we have, from our money to our bodies and emotionality. Ever since I began to like guys, I thought that if I was not in a relationship then I wasn't living my best life. I was incomplete, a failure. This is one of the biggest lies that young women have been force-fed and fall for all the time.

Along this journey, we have lost who we are to the point where our highest goal in life is a relationship with a man. We have lost our identity as "woman," as God's image bearer and have taken on this false and crippling identity of "man pleaser."

While you are worried about whether a guy likes your body or not, God is saying, "I created your body for my purpose and pleasure, not his." We have been too busy trying to lift up a man's penis instead of lifting up the name of God in all His splendor!

 #TheGirlfriendTrap

> *We have been too busy trying to lift up a man's penis instead of lifting up the name of God in all His splendor!*

#TheGirlfriendTrap

When do we begin to care more about growing in womanhood and building our minds? When do we start increasing in knowledge of God and self, seeking the good of others, and helping to raise up the next generation to be good stewards of their bodies and God-given gifts?

Let me tell you why you even desire a relationship with the opposite sex: because God gave you that desire. But it's not for your own selfish pleasures or to fix your own brokenness left by an absent father or a previous guy. It has been given to you so that you may prepare to be in a committed marriage that will tell the world about God and his love, commitment, selflessness, faithfulness, forgiveness, grace, mercy and so forth. If you desire to be with a guy without God and His desires being at the center of that relationship, then it's a desire birthed from lust that will be your downfall in the end.

When that desire is awakened, it does not mean jump into a relationship with the first guy you think is cute. It means you are now ready to learn what it means to be a wife. You are now ready to sit at the feet of a mature woman and learn from her servanthood. You are now ready for the next level in maturation on how to worship a Holy King. It's time to grow up!

Save Yourself

A big part of growth and maturation is learning how to save yourself. Have you ever saved a lot of money to make a big purchase? Maybe it was your first pair of designer shoes, your first car, and for some, even a home. You had a game plan in place. You knew that it was going to take a certain amount of money and even more discipline on your end if you were going to be able to purchase it. What would happen if you decided to spend that money on much smaller items along the way, items that were not as valuable but satisfying for the moment? Right, you would not have enough money to buy what you had originally set your heart on having.

You are going to need every bit of your self-esteem, emotionality, mental health and physical wholeness to be the best version of yourself for servanthood. Why servanthood? Because mature women serve their homes, communities and the world. You were created to live a selfless life not a "selfie" life and to do that you are going to have to value and appreciate yourself much more than what you do now. You can't afford to spend yourself along the way on every guy who says they like you or excites your senses for a moment.

Girl, no matter how fine he is, no matter how funny or fly you think he is, you have a bigger goal in mind. If he has not proven himself to be a man after God's heart who will partner with you to lift God up, then let his fine, funny and fly self walk straight on by. You can either spend yourself on an imposter and lose a life's savings, or you can be patient and wise and invest yourself in the right one when that time comes, and get a bigger return than what you put in to start with. The only romantic relationship where that can happen is marriage.

Wait, does that sound a little crazy? Are you thinking, "that's too much too soon." If you are, trust me, I understand why. But this is in fact the path to travel. Purity of heart, sexual integrity and the pursuit of purpose has been trampled and killed in our dating culture. We have been so desensitized and removed from commitment that we actually prefer to stay broken and waste time. We would rather play house than prepare for a real relationship of commitment where godly assignments are completed, and that has to change. So, let's start now.

How do you go from wasting your life with a guy to attracting a quality guy that you can make the greatest and best investment in through marriage?

Simple, by dating…the RIGHT way!

The History of Dating

Dating is still a fairly new concept here in our western civilization. According to a New York Post article, *The fascinating history of how courtship became 'dating'* by Larry Getlen, dating became a thing at the end of the 1800s going into the early 1900's. As women began to seek economical and social freedoms, they saw this as a sense of independence and felt the need to spread that independence to other areas of their lives, like when it came to engaging with men. This need for freedom was pursued due to oppressive mindsets and behaviors from their culture and authoritative male figures in their lives who did not truly know the beauty and power that a woman possesses.

#TheGirlfriendTrap

Sleeping around with whoever you want does not make you free. It makes you bound and a slave to your sinful desires just as much as the man who is doing the same thing.

#TheGirlfriendTrap

Because of that, I believe as women sought out certain freedoms, they forsook the structure of the home and family dynamic, which was never intended to be bondage but protection. This is what happens when men suppress or abuse women in any kind of way. Women tend to lash out in the name of freedom, not realizing that they go on to freely choose a different kind of oppression. We see it in our feminist movement today. Sleeping around with whoever you want does not make you free. It makes you bound and a slave to your sinful desires just as much as the man who is doing the same thing.

Before dating, there was the practice of prearranged marriages and courting, which added structure to the lives of the 2 young people being brought together.

As more and more women began to no longer depend solely on their fathers or a husband for income and stability, it gave birth to women seeking financial security in other ways. Back then, women were not nearly paid as much as men were, so they had to make up that difference elsewhere. They began to seek out men for favors, like having men take them out and pay for their food and entertainment. In return, women would give the men favors, many times through sex. This is why till this day, when some guys treat women on dates, they expect sexual favors in return.

As this dating practice grew, prostitutes became angry at women who dated because these dating women were taking their clients from them and having sex with them "for free," well, really in exchange for dinner or a good time out on the town, but you get what I mean. Back then, dating was initially coined as someone filling up someone else's dates on a calendar, and in the 1800's, if that word was discussed, it was only in regards to prostitution. This explains why today, most, if not all, your dating relationships turn to sexual relationships. Most women have sex not in exchange for money but in exchange for feeling loved, feeling wanted or to try to fill a deep void that she is not aware that she has.

When you seek after illegal sex (sex in disobedience to God's word) that is a symptom of a deeper issue. Your soul is telling you that you are void of deep intimacy and connection, and you sense that it needs to be filled. Unfortunately, due to the average young woman's ignorance, she mistakenly thinks that this desire for connection means to have sex, when it really means seek after God with all your heart. Illegal sex never fulfills a man or woman's need for intimacy because sex can't fill what only God can.

"For this is the will of God, your sanctification: that you abstain from sexual immorality; that each one of you know how to control his own body in holiness and honor, not in the passion of lust like the Gentiles who do not know God; that no one transgress and wrong his brother in this matter, because the Lord is an avenger in all these things, as we told you beforehand and solemnly

warned you. For God has not called us for impurity, but in holiness. Therefore whoever disregards this, disregards not man but God, who gives his Holy Spirit to you. – **1 Thessalonians 4:3-8 (ESV)**

This Scripture shows us that people who don't know God for themselves engage in illegal sex. When you seek after God and God alone and you truly get to know Him and allow Him to fill you with everything good, you won't have a need to seek after illegal sex. I know from my own life struggles and sexual addictions that most of our illegal sexual practices are because God's Spirit is not the only spirit we engage with or we don't seek to be filled by Him in everything we do. We don't engage with God's spirit alone but with demonic spirits, which prevent us from fully knowing God intimately and knowing God only. I just wanted to share that small piece of info as this is definitely a conversation for another day. Let's get back on topic

As the act of dating grew, the input from family and the structured and supervised visits of the two involved became less and less. Because of that, morals quickly faded as well. What used to be seen as vile and obscene quickly became normal and just mere fun. Before dating, marriage was the goal for any 2 people coming together. As dating evolved, that quickly became less of a desire and just coming together to have fun became the goal. Before dating, having feelings for one another and the idea of "falling in love," were never involved when a young man was pursuing another man's daughter. After dating came on the scene, feelings and "falling in love" became the primary motivators in a dating relationship. They quickly took the place of sound wisdom that parents infused to make sure a young woman was paired with a suitable life partner, economically, socially and spiritually.

Dating became the preferred way of engaging with men because it was freedom from rules and structure. While most people still see it this way, I see the diabolical plan that the enemy has been unfolding since the birth of evil, the removal of the father. Our cultural dating was and still is a way of removing the voice and covering of the father from the daughter, causing her to be unprotected, lost and confused out here on the dating scene. Because of this removal, women are the most battered and bruised gender in the world of dating. The average young woman has no clue of what she is doing while dating. She is used and manipulated for sex, cooking and cleaning, for her resources, whether it be money or a free ride, and in the end, she is tossed back into the sea, only to be caught by yet another predator looking for a quick meal.

The most dangerous position that a woman can be in while dating is in an uncovered position with no father and no wise counsel surrounding and insulating her.

"Likewise, husbands, live with your wives in an understanding way, showing honor to the woman as the weaker vessel, since they are heirs with you of the grace of life, so that your prayers may not be hindered." – **1 Peter 3:7 (ESV)**

We as women are the weaker vessel in comparison to men. This is not an attack on our value, intelligence, ability to produce, lead, create nor innovate. In fact, it's not an attack at all but an accurate statement. The physical frame of a woman was never designed to carry the weight of that of a man. We as women are also softer in heart. We are the heart of the world and lead in softness and nurture while men are the strength and lead in might and protection.

> 66 #TheGirlfriendTrap
>
> *The most dangerous position that a woman can be in while dating is in an uncovered position with no father and no wise counsel surrounding and insulating her.*
>
> #TheGirlfriendTrap 99

The devil knew that if he could get to the heart of the woman, away from her covering, then he could dismantle her strength and protection. This is why the devil tempted Eve, not Adam, in the Garden of Eden and was able to successfully deceive her.

Now the serpent was more crafty than any other beast of the field that the Lord God had made. He said to the woman, "Did God actually say, 'You shall not eat of any tree in the garden'?" – **Genesis 3:1 (ESV)**

The heart of a woman is easier to penetrate and be swayed when it's not protected because it naturally looks to anyone who appears to have power and authority and will submit to them in hopes of being protected. The devil knew that the heart of a man could be more easily deceived if a woman brought about the deception instead of him because the woman has the power to get a man to let his guard down quicker than anything else in the world. This is why the devil did not attempt to deceive Adam first but did it through the woman, a cowardly move. And when that happened, the family structure slowly began to unravel.

If the move worked, then why change it? If the devil can get to the woman's heart outside of her protection, then it's downhill from there. The younger she is, the better. Why not encourage women to think that they would live a more fun and free life if they didn't have a father guiding and watching over them. The father of the average young woman doesn't even know that she is dating let alone who she is dating. She doesn't even consult with Father God first before talking to a guy and that's down right scary.

"Why do I need to include my father in my dating life?"

The question that every young woman defiantly asks with pride and ignorance. It's the same deception that we continue to accept. I would like to share with you practical evidence to show how we have bitten into that lie. Our modern dating culture tells us that we are ready to date based on the silliest reasons imaginable, and these are reasons outside of the guidance and protection of an intentional father. Some of those reasons are:

1. You turned 16 or 18
2. You like a guy
3. You go to the same school
4. You're bored
5. You feel lonely
6. You are reaching a certain age

7. You want to get "experience"
8. You want a free meal
9. You want to have sex
10. You need a place to live
11. You feel you guys look good together.

These are all surface and causal reasons for dating that will almost always leave you single or a single mother and broken-hearted in the end. (shout out to ALL single mothers by the way. Your value is not diminished in the slightest way. I'm just stating facts). If any young woman were to go to her natural father or Father God and say that she is ready to date based on any of those reasons, I would hope that he would respond with this question or something similar, "What does that have to do with your future life stability, assignments from God and your worship to Him?"

That question shows you that these reasons are not sturdy or intentional enough to begin a dating relationship. Anything built on them will crumble, as I'm sure it already has. Some better reasons to consider when determining if you are ready to date are:

1. You have an intimate relationship with Father God.
2. You know your personal purpose/assignment here on earth
3. You have acquired biblical knowledge on why God made a woman for a man in the first place.
4. You know the beauty and power of prayer and holiness.
5. You have learned the purpose and worthiness of servanthood and a gentle and quiet spirit.
6. You understand the purpose and joy of sex, **the reasons for reserving sex for commitment**, building a home and the mission that God has called man and woman to embark upon together.
7. You can successfully engage in basic life management skills such as managing money, preparing healthy food and cleaning your living space.

All those other reasons fail in comparison to these, as it should, because dating a guy and allowing him to pursue you romantically is no light or casual thing. Your heart is at stake and that's worth stepping back and reassessing your true readiness to date.

A portion of my assignment from God is to teach the young woman the importance of being covered by a father figure and/or Father God because without that covering, the woman's heart is deceived, trampled on, manipulated, battered and wounded. And when that woman gives birth to children, they will end up the same way, because most of the time there's no covering for them either. The vicious cycle continues. The goal is to keep the young woman's heart covered and protected, whether she stays single and never gets married or enters a healthy God-centered marriage.

As much as I would love to throw our dating culture in the trash and start over, I know it would be like me trying to push a whole mountain with my bare hands. Instead, I'm going to chisel away at it, little by little by giving the average young woman proper knowledge and strategy that she can use as she prepares to step onto the dating scene. As a woman who has successfully got out of the trap, I am going to teach you how to do the same, never entering one again, by sharing with you a better approach to dating altogether.

What I am about to share with you is dating that introduces structure and ultimately the father's direction and protection. If you grab hold of this wisdom, pace yourself and use self-control in the process, you will set yourself up for physical, emotional and spiritual success for a lifetime.

Put Dating Back in Its Place

How does one date? **You start by putting dating back into its proper place which is under the covering of a father/father figure and within the structure of family and accountability**. The reason why we as women suffer so much when dating is because we have taken dating out of its proper place and have isolated it and used it the wrong way. You can't take a phone battery out of the phone and expect the phone to work properly. The same goes for dating. It just does not work that way. And I'm glad it doesn't. Using things in the right way teaches us how to live in order and follow directions, something we desperately need training on.

Before we go any further, I would like to introduce to you courtship or courting, which is of great importance in this discussion of dating.

Courting means to win someone's favor with the intention to marry them, according to the Oxford English Dictionary. Here is a simpler definition: **To date with the intention to marry.**

Courting and dating are very similar but different at the same time. What makes them similar is that they both include the concept of dating. What makes them different is that one is dating within structure, boundaries, protection and has a purposeful and productive end goal while the other has none of that. With those differences that I just stated, the biggest difference between our modern approach to dating and the process of courting is the absence or presence of a father.

Here is a great explanation of courting vs. dating shared by Scott Croft from the book, *Sex and the Supremacy of Christ.*

Dating

"Dating, a more modern approach, begins when either the man or the woman initiates a more-than-friends relationship with the other, and then they conduct that relationship outside of any oversight or authority. Dating may or may not have marriage as its goal."

Courting

"Courtship ordinarily begins when a single man approaches a single woman by going through the woman's father, and then conducts his relationship with the woman under the authority of her father, family, or church, whichever is most appropriate. Courtship always has marriage as its direct goal."

When it comes to romantic relationships, the only purpose that you should have as a wise or becoming wise woman is to pursue marriage. Why else would you spend time in conversation and invest in a guy to a certain degree if not to pursue something with intention and purpose? Dating for any other reason will lead to sin and settling, I guarantee you.

Courting is the ultimate testing of your (and/or your father's) belief that a person is marriage material suitable for your needs and your God given assignment and vice versa. The end of the courting process is you both deciding that you can entrust your life to one another in marriage or not. Period!

As you court, you are vying to win each other's favor with the intent to marry, and you do that by actually dating each other. Dating someone simply means to gather data about them. I will explain in more detail what dating should look like. But first, I want to introduce to you 2 concepts of dating that I believe will help you have a better grasp on what it looks like to pursue the opposite sex for future commitment and companionship. They are pre-dating and post-dating.

Pre-dating is the information you gather about an individual BEFORE courtship begins, while post-dating is what you continue to gather AFTER the courting process has begun.

Pre-dating, let's call it casual dating, is the information that you gather in a casual setting about the person. Although you are gathering data, the person does not need to necessarily know that you are doing it. That's why I call it casual, because it's not something that is defined between the two of you. For example, if a guy sends a message to my inbox on social media confessing an interest in me, I can immediately begin to gather data about him (pre-date). This may look like me assessing how he approached me and the words he used, which says a lot about his character, or what he posts on his social media and so forth. If I knew this guy in a real setting, like at school or within a shared community, it could be the everyday info I gather about him by just observing and listening to him. If a guy tells me that he is an atheist, I just gathered info about him that tells me that there is no way on earth that he would ever be marriage material for me. The pre-dating info you gather will determine if you should court this guy or not, if it gets to that point.

Post-dating, let's call it serious dating, is the info you gather about him during the courting phase. This is after he has spoken to your father/family structure to ask for favor to pursue you with the hopes of marriage. This data is gathered with great intention and diligence all within the pursuit of marriage.

Look at it like this; pre-dating determines if he is worthy of courting will post-dating further helps you decide if he is worthy of marriage. Before you get to the courting phase, there should already be signs that lets you know that he is marriage material. If not, then there is no point in courting him.

Both dating concepts start under the covering of a father/ father figure. Don't miss this. Even during pre-dating, if you decide that you are going to pursue something more with this guy who has shared an interest in you, you need your protection in place. I often hear stories of young women thinking that they can pre-date alone, talk more and get closer to the guy, but won't bring the guy around her father/family until she "feels" that it's serious enough to do so. As I understand the idea, it's not wise to keep your father in the dark at any stage, because it's in the nonserious or pre-dating phase that boundaries are crossed, soul ties are made, and pregnancies happen. This is because, yet again, she is dating outside a covering.

Dating has been taken out of place and you have a responsibility to put it back where it belongs. A father should be involved as quickly as possible, even if it's just sharing the guy's name, what he is saying to you and if you have an interest in him as well. If you don't have an interest in him then don't even bother sharing, simply toss him.

Trust me, this is wisdom speaking to you. Doing this will shed a light on or expose anything dark from the jump and you need the exposure to happen. Even if there is nothing to expose, this process should not be hidden or in isolation. **The girlfriend trap is undefeated** and the evil spirits behind the trap will find any kind of way to get you into it. Be wiser than the enemy by letting others into your dating life.

Let me show you a brief comparison of what happens when you place dating underneath an umbrella of protection vs. taking it from underneath it.

Dating Under Protection

Dating Outside Protection

Do you see the difference? Relationships don't last or become broken because they start off wrong and most of the time when it starts off wrong it ends…wrong! Once you understand the importance and value in dating as a covered and protected woman, it's time to not just talk about it but actively be about it.

If you have a healthy father figure who makes good decisions that can lead and guide you, get underneath his covering and allow him to protect you during this process. That means telling him about your interest in dating and allowing him to walk with you as your wisdom and guidance through these murky waters, and I do mean murky. A father's job is to protect his daughter, and that he will do until the day he dies. In order for him to do that, he has to be aware of any potential danger that may be lurking, and that's going to be contingent on your willingness to be open and free with him. Honor his God-given mandate to protect you. Don't hide from him or try to be secretive in any way. That is a foolish and immature thing to do as you will block out good judgment and ultimately your protection.

Remember, any guy who wants to pursue you needs to be checked and vetted. He needs to know that there is a father who is watching out for you and watching his every move no matter what age you are. He needs to be held accountable for his words and actions toward you. When there is no father around, guys are more prone to disrespect you verbally and physically by having sex with you, because there is no one there to instill the fear of God in him. Every guy needs to sense and be aware of the reality that you are not his to touch, and God uses fathers to make that reality known.

What does that look like, you ask? How does a young woman incorporate her father into her dating life? What do you say to him? What if you don't have a good father figure in your life? Don't worry, there is a strategy for it all, and I answer these questions and more in my book, 35 *Tips on How to Win at Dating*. This book will help you continue your dating preparation and reveal to you some amazing dating tips that you definitely want to know.

As you run for cover, understand that your father is just the first to go to for help. In some instances, a father may be all you need and desire to be a part of your dating life and that's okay. But for many, a whole squad of wisdom may be necessary, and I encourage it. God blesses us with different relationships to help round all of our sharp edges and give us different perspectives that speak to the complexities, levels and stages of our lives.

A conversation with a woman will be different than a conversation with a man, as it should be. Men can't always speak to everything that a woman experiences, like our menstrual cycles, for example. This is where mothers or women elders come in. If you have other family members that you trust for sound wisdom, don't hesitate to glean from them. Sometimes, friends can definitely be that extra wise voice as well, but I say sometimes because not every friend is wise. Some friends are in the same ditch that you may be in, so it makes no sense to go to them for wisdom that they don't have yet, or possibly will never have.

How to Date

What you have been doing is not dating at all. You are used to liking a guy and him liking you (or what you can do for him), claiming each other as boyfriend and girlfriend and then getting trapped there. The reason why it has not worked out for you is because you didn't know the true meaning of dating which prevented you from dating with morals and dignity.

As stated before, the proper definition of dating means to *gather data* about the opposite sex, and I would add on, with the purpose of identifying compatibility and furthering the relationship. You are much more familiar with dating than you think. Any time you pursue information about someone you're interested in, it's dating. It can be a person you met at a gathering, or a new neighbor who just moved onto your street. It can even be your classmate, a coworker, etc. If you are having any length of conversation with a guy you're interested in, discovering new things about him: who he is, where he's from, his character, how you both measure up to one another, then you are engaging in dating.

When you obtain information about a person, whether you realize it or not, you are making many small assessments in your head about them. We will get more into what it truly means to assess someone, but a quick definition of assess is to evaluate or estimate the nature, ability, or quality of something, says Oxford's English Dictionaries. The issue is, when it comes to dating the opposite sex, young women are not as thorough of daters as they should be, and they end up misassessing or not assessing guys at all for the matter. This leads to many young women suffering from their poor dating choices. This all happens because most young women date with no purpose or end goal in mind. Now that we have decided to date as a covered woman, this immature way of dating should dwindle and cease.

When dating, your first conversation with a guy may not be that deep and you may not know where the conversation will go. Despite that, you should already have clearly defined goals and expectations that you have created for yourself which gives you clarity and shows you where you are headed in life. Even if, for some odd reason, a guy doesn't make his intentions with you as clear, which is a red flag by the way, and a guy like that should have NEVER got past the father check; you should be clear on who you are and where you are going.

Some of those goals may be to:

1. Develop and maintain a strong and solid relationship with God.
2. Start a business.
3. Pursue ministry of some sort.
4. Finish school.
5. Get/keep a steady job.
6. Save a large amount of money.
7. Become an author.
8. Have good and healthy friendships/relationships with people.
9. Become a professional_____
10. Be a person of integrity and live an honest life.
11. Live a life of sexual integrity (reserve sex for marriage).
12. Become a wife to a husband.
13. Start a family with your husband, etc.

Having goals already sets you apart from the average dating young woman because the average young woman has no defined goals, and because she has no defined goals, she is not intentional with dating. Intention means to do something with an end goal in mind. Your clearly defined goals for yourself should make you an intentional dater, and if anyone presents themselves as a threat to any of your goals, then you should not date them.

For example, it makes no sense to date a guy who has no desire to grow with God because it opposes your goal in being close to God. That would be considered a poor dating choice. It also makes no sense to date a liar or someone who is not interested in sexual integrity and commitment if your goal is honesty and marriage. Your life goals don't blend with his which will create a catastrophe of a relationship. Your goals automatically make you an intentional dater and because you have intention, you will assess any guy you date to see if they line up with your goals and have intention as well.

If you find it hard to be intentional, a good and solid question to ask yourself when starting a dating relationship with a guy is, "why are we talking?" It may shock you that most people who are dating cannot answer this question with clarity. I could never answer this question because, truthfully, I dated all wrong, and I never had a good reason as to why I dated any guy I was ever involved with. When I was immature, I had no other reason to date than to fill my voids, and I had no clarity of what I wanted out of life outside of my broken heart.

Let's say your response to that question is, "to get to know each other," it automatically brings the next question, "Once you know each other, then what?" This question must be asked because, again, when it comes to dating, there should be an end goal in mind. No one meets with another person on a consistent basis without there being some sort of end goal. Even business partners have lunch dates with an end goal in mind, to make money.

So what do you want? What is the purpose of you talking to this guy?

Note: If you are having a hard time discovering this, plan out a brainstorming session with Father God of course, your father figure, family and or trusted circle to help you discover who you are and what you desire so that you can have more clarity going forward.

Let me show you some examples of just how intentional and goal-oriented you have already been.

1. You talk to your teacher so that you can get help on an assignment to pass a class.
2. You talk to the cashier so that you can make a transaction to pay for your items.
3. You talk to the mailman/woman to see if they have your package.
4. You talk to your parents to get the wisdom that they have acquired over life so that you can do life better.
5. You talk to strangers to sell a product, get quick information to them or from them, to recruit them, pray for them, etc.
6. You talk to friends to build social skills and exchange information.
7. You talk to a pastor to gain spiritual insight as you strengthen your relationship with God.
8. You talk to God to get to know Him, ask Him for help and to discover and fulfill your assignments here on earth.

When it comes to talking to a guy, there should be just as much purpose and intention as the rest of your conversations. Why? Because a conversation with no purpose is a conversation with no boundaries. Conversations like this open the door to lies, manipulation, sex, confusion, abuse, bondage and when things like this come into play, you will end up in a ditch somewhere...trapped.

> #TheGirlfriendTrap
>
> *A conversation with no purpose is a conversation with no boundaries.*
>
> #TheGirlfriendTrap

Let's take a look at this scripture that speaks to what I just said.

"When there are many words, transgression and offense are unavoidable. But he who controls his lips and keeps thoughtful silence is wise." – Proverbs 10:19 (AMP)

What this Scripture means is the more words exchanged with a person, the more likely sin and some level of disrespect will happen. But a person who has self-control, who is intentional and places boundaries around their words toward another is wise, even if that means stopping the conversation with that person all together because you realize there is no purpose for the relationship or the words being exchanged.

Culture has told us that dating is an "all in" kind of thing, but it's quite the opposite. Until this guy can assume a legit role in your life, that being husband, you should always engage with care and caution. You don't need to put a title on him. In fact, **you don't even need to label this guy as anything in your life at all because only time will tell what this guy will become to you**. That means when someone asks you "who is he?" you don't lead with what he is to you but what you are doing with him. Instead of saying, "this is my…," you say, "this is (his name) and we are courting." The only thing you need to call him is his name, and the only things you need to date him is your mouth, to speak, and a notepad and a pen to record data.

> **#TheGirlfriendTrap**
>
> *Your job is to gather information about him and that's it!*
>
> **#TheGirlfriendTrap**

Your job is to gather information about him and that's it! Tell me, queen, where do feelings come into play? Where does touching and kissing come into play? Where does spending the night and even sex come into play? It doesn't…at all! All of that just gets in the way. It clouds your judgment and hinders your job of gathering as much data about him as possible.

This leads to the topic of boundaries. A boundary is "a visible mark indicating a dividing line, a limit or furthest point of extension of any one thing," says Online Etymology Dictionary. I want you to highlight the word "visible" in that definition. If that line has not been clearly drawn out and defined, if the other person can't verbally say what your boundaries are, then you have not drawn any boundaries. Boundaries must be known and understood between both of you. Boundaries are the roadblocks that you have to place in any and every dating relationship because, like any boundary, they keep a person from going somewhere that they don't need to go or don't have permission to go. Hear me, queen, if you don't have adequate boundaries in place, I guarantee you that a guy will gain access to your heart quickly and your heart will be injured in some kind of way.

During a dating relationship, this guy has no rights, and I mean no rights, to anything that is valuable or permanent in your life. This includes, your body, your house, your car, your money, your passwords, your phone, your social security number, your social media accounts, your kids, etc. Do you get my drift? Boundaries protect all those things from harm, loss and theft. You do not give a guy access to any of those things until he has proven himself trustworthy and capable to protect and honor those things. When is that? Marriage! Why? Because marriage is the ultimate act of commitment, trust and protection.

When a guy marries you, he is saying he is investing everything he has in you. He is giving up his independent life to have a joint life with you. That means whatever he does to you, he will be doing to himself. No sane person will intentionally harm himself which means he will also treat everything concerning you with the utmost care. This is generally speaking. Not every guy who marries a woman cares about her. This is why studying his character while dating is key because no one can hide the true nature of their heart for too long.

Boundaries need to be set in place before a dating relationship ever starts. Here are the types of boundaries that you will need to put in place.

1. Verbal
2. Social
3. Mental
4. Emotional
5. Physical
6. Spiritual

To go in depth with each boundary, purchase my book, *35 Tips on How to Win at Dating*.

What Dating Looks Like

There are many ways you can gather data about someone. It can be in social gatherings, maybe you are at a friend's house and the guy that you are interested in is there. Even listening to how he speaks in a relaxing setting like that is a way to collect information about him. And might I add, one of the best ways, because you get to experience him in his natural element with no pressure to put on or try to present the best and sometimes dishonest version of himself.

It can be at a restaurant as you engage in a good meal. How does he interact with the people that work there? How does he treat the waitress? How does he interact with you? With money? Is he polite? Does he open doors for you or even other strangers? Does he have masculine energy that shows he protects women and does not objectify them or use them? Does he pay for the meal? Which does not mean he is romantically invested in you, but simply that he knows how to treat a young woman.

When it comes to me and my people, we teach young men to always treat women with care and respect, that includes paying the tab. Whether it's a brother taking his little sister out to eat or a son treating one of the women elders in our family, we believe it is the man's chivalrous duty to honor a woman in this way. Why? Because it teaches and reinforces his role as a provider and protector of women. These small data collections give you insight into his mind, even if he doesn't share these things with you word for word.

As stated before, you can also collect data through social media. Thank you, technology! Although people try to present a fake version of themselves online, it can still tell you a lot about a person. Who does he follow? That tells you how he is influenced. What kind of language does he share? That tells you what's in his heart. Does he follow a lot of women who post naked pictures? That tells you how he views women and/or possible lust issues he may have. These are just a few things that his public life reveals.

Of course, one way to gather data is good ole talking on the phone, that's if he actually talks instead of texting. If all he does is text, girl, let that little boy go play on the playground somewhere. I just saved you from wasting your time. Talking on the phone is more intentional and has the potential of revealing a lot about a person as there are less distractions to get past and more attention to give to detail.

Now, I will say this. **When a man gets access to your ears, that is a gateway to your heart.** I repeat! When a man gets access to your ears, that is a direct gateway to your heart. Queen, be careful who you let get this kind of access. This is why it's so important that you have other people, preferably a father/another man, vet this guy out to make sure he isn't a crazy person, predator or shyster. You also want to make sure that your heart is reinforced with the word of God because **once a guy has your ear, he can sway your heart, like the devil did Eve in the garden of Eden. If you are easily swayed and talked out of your panties, then you do NOT need to be dating anyone right now, let alone talking to him on the phone. Please go heal and soak in the word of God…immediately!**

When talking on the phone, does he show interest in getting to know you? Can he hold a conversation? Does he ask meaningful questions, like, what is your family dynamic? Do you have any dreams or aspirations? What is your relationship like with God, etc.?

Pay attention to what he asks you. This will tell how serious or nonchalant he is when it comes to getting to know you as a young woman. Again, the point of dating is to gather information, not see who can "fall in love" first.

Speaking of that, I want to highlight a concept that my mentor talks about often. Falling in love is a culture-based approach to romance, and there is no such thing as falling into anything that must be intentionally pursued. God is love, and with God, you must get to know Him. When you know Him, only then can you make a decision to be in a relationship with Him. When have you ever known someone or yourself to fall and not say "ouch?" No one falls on purpose, and if they do, it's generally because they lost balance and control. We all have control over who we decide to engage with, and the concept of falling in love takes away your self-control and ability to choose as a human. These two things are very important when it comes to dating.

The A.T.P Dating Method

When you begin to gather data about a guy, you will immediately begin to notice how he operates. This will help you categorize him and the sooner you can do this the better. I'd like to introduce to you the A.T.P dating method which is a way to categorize every guy you find interest in. When I came up with this method, I had no clue that the acronym would come out to be A.T.P, which is amazing because it's exactly what's needed to keep women out of the trap. To understand what I mean, let's take a small dip into science. Don't worry, we won't be here long.

I have a B.S. in Clinical Laboratory Sciences, and as you can imagine, we had to learn about all things science. A big portion of that was learning biochemistry. Do you know what ATP is in the science world? It stands for Adenosine triphosphate, and it is what our bodies produce, after we feed it, to provide energy for every cellular process. It is referred to as the fuel of life, and without ATP, the human body would not function right and cells would begin to die. When there is no ATP, there is no movement, and that's what I want you to take away from this short trip to science land. ATP is energy and energy fuels movement.

As you date, you are going to need a constant flow of energy and the goal of dating is to keep moving, eventually moving to a clean ending of the dating relationship or all the way to marriage. That doesn't mean you will make it to marriage with the first guy you date or even the one you are dating now but understand the purpose here. If you are not ready to get married, then you should not be seriously dating anyone. What sense does it make to start a dating relationship with someone to go absolutely nowhere?

This A.T.P dating method provides that energy for movement, eliminating chances of getting trapped along the dating journey. Each letter stands for a category, and when dating any guy, you should be able to place him in one of them. The goal is to categorize a guy during the pre-dating phase so that you only post-date a guy that is truly marriage material. Either way, if a guy makes it to a serious dating phase with you and you discover that you categorized him wrong, you can always shift him into another category so that you can know what to do with him and save yourself time and energy. Two of these categories ultimately bring the dating relationship to an end and one of them keeps you and him in motion. Can you tell which one it is?

A= Assignment
T= Throw Away
P= Potential

Assignment

Every guy that you are attracted to is not meant for you. Sometimes, you may be attracted to a guy because you both are from the same hometown, you have the same interest in music, you vibe well or because there needs to be a positive exchange between you two. Attraction does not always mean, "I need to date you," but it could mean, "I need to be a witness to you." There are times when you will meet a guy and the only purpose you have with him is to show him the love, kindness and standard of God. We live in a world where men are trained from youth to objectify women. It's embedded in our culture. It's in our music videos, advertisements, and don't get me started on the porn industry.

It takes a man to teach a boy how to be a man and to value, honor and respect women. If a guy meets you before he encounters that man, then queen, you are going to have to school him for the time being. If you have not already, now would be the best time to place a crown on top of your head. This category is huge because this is the category where women get guys confused with the potential category, and I've gotten a few confused myself.

I remember meeting a guy, and over a period of time, he would flirt with me, and I would invite his flirtatious behavior. He was very charismatic, and I really liked engaging with him. He always made me laugh, and I let the guard of my heart down without even realizing it. One day, I had a real conversation with him, and he pulled a straight up clown move on me. I asked him what this flirting was all about, and he told me he was involved with another young woman, but if that fell through, then he would hit me up.

Wait, excuse me? Who the heck do you think I am? Whoever you think I am, you better think again, playboy!

I learned a lesson right then and there; just because he was attracted to me, and I was attracted to him didn't mean that I was supposed to take it any further. I later found out that he slept with girls as a sport, and he had been on his one-man team for years.

When it came to me, he had the right one, because even if he thought I was about to be another notch on his belt, he had another thing coming. I soon realized that this guy was dealing with a specific evil spirit that even tried to torment me in my dreams. I later went on to give him some much-needed truth from a young woman's heart, and I let it be known that as long as I was in the same vicinity as him, he would have no chance with me or even be allowed to interact with me how I previously allowed him to. Actually, I stopped talking to the guy all together outside of exchanging normal greetings. I created a standard that was unwavering, and that standard was a witness to him. You are called to do the same thing.

One of the biggest clues you will get from guys to let you know that he is an assignment is him being far from God. He will either say it with his mouth or show it in his actions. Your job from that moment on is to pray for him and keep it moving.

Like any assignment you have ever done in school, it had instructions and a due date. Same here. After you pray for him, you must submit him to your teacher, God. Assignments are not for you to hold on to but to give over to God, and He will assess your work and give you feedback. If you have ever held on to an assignment longer than what you should have, then you will know that it causes deductions from your grade and if you never turn your assignment in, well then, you fail.

Oftentimes, we take losses in our hearts because we hold on to guys too long when we should have turned him over to God much sooner. And of course, there are situations where we never turn him in, suffering the consequences of it too. We quickly experience that his deficiencies don't meet the necessary standards of survival for a relationship. Had we submitted him to God, He would have told us that, instead of us having to learn the hard way.

> 66 #TheGirlfriendTrap
>
> *Turn in your assignment. Don't screw your assignment.*
>
> #TheGirlfriendTrap 99

I heard a great teacher, Apostle Bryan Meadows, say that we often end up having sex with our assignment because of our unchecked, unrestrained and selfish feelings. Unfortunately, it's true! And by his words, I'm here to encourage you to turn in your assignment. Don't screw your assignment.

Another instruction for your assignment may even be to share with the guy some good male mentors that you know. That way you eliminate any false responsibilities you may be tempted to put on yourself concerning him. We women have a strong tendency to try to save, fix and mold guys to our liking, hoping that if he changes, we would be able to date him in the near future. This is what you call evangelistic dating and it's a bad move and wrong motive. That's a selfish move, one that cares more about what you want instead of what he needs as a human, which is God.

What that looks like is you trying to mother him. Let me pop that bubble for you real quick! You are not his mother nor are you called to raise him, provide for him, coddle him, or even fight for him. If he is showing a need for the basic necessities, lead him to resources that can help him, just like you would a stranger you just met. That's a hard boundary line that you must draw, but it's necessary because there is nothing worse than carrying the weight of a mother for a grown man. Even wives don't do that. That's where elders, therapists, counselors and the like come in.

If you continue and date a guy who is in need of some serious direction, not only will you be putting your heart in danger, but you will be hindering his growth with God. He needs no distractions on his path to God, especially if that distraction is you. A man without the know-how to achieve the basic needs is a man with poor management and leadership skills. He does not need a woman; he needs a man to teach him. He needs instructions from the Lord, and a man with no instructions from the Lord can only lead you to himself, the bed, a backseat, it's all the same.

You may also be attracted to a guy because you both have the same, hurts, wounds and traumas in common. Most boyfriend-girlfriend relationships happen based on this attraction. I was a hurt and rejected young woman and because of that, I attracted the same kind as me. This is a form of trauma bonding. I didn't know it at the time, but I was looking for my father, and I attracted a young man who was looking for his mother. We both had parent wounds and when we got together, we became a wounded dynamic duo. I remember there were times when I actually cradled this guy like a mother would a son, and I held onto him like a little girl would hold onto her father. We wouldn't let each other go because we pacified each other's wounds, thinking we were helping each other, but in reality, we were hurting each other more.

This is the danger in dating while wounded. You will make the wound worse while getting further and further from the one who can actually heal you, God. How do you know you are dating while wounded? When you begin to feel like you need a guy to fulfill some part of you. Another sign is when a guy walks away from you (or the thought of it) and a part of you feels torn, distraught or empty, to the point where you will do anything just to get him back. You more than likely have a rejection wound, and only Father God can heal it. Healed people can stand being single because they know God's presence alone is fulfilling with or without a romantic relationship.

"He heals the brokenhearted, and binds up their wounds." – **Psalm 147:3 (ESV)**

That is not the only indication that you are wounded, but I believe it's the most common and detectable one. If this is you right now, I encourage you to let go of any guy you are talking to and stop dating for the time being. You should then turn your attention inward. That guy just showed you that you are also the assignment and that you need to go to God for your own healing before putting yourself back out there onto the dating scene.

Throw Away

This category is pretty easy and straightforward. This is the guy you come across that is straight up belligerent, disrespectful and is only looking for a hole to stick his penis in. He has no sense of self-respect let alone any respect for you. When it comes to guys like this, they immediately give you a bad feeling. Do not ignore this feeling and do not pass go. Girl, run!

These are the guys that meet your booty and breast before they meet you. They have already decided what they want to do with you before you ever open your mouth to speak a word. They may even say derogatory things to you about your body or private parts and you have to fight to reject that type of disrespect. Do not internalize it as something cute or believe that's just what guys do or say. No, that's what boys do, immature and disrespectful boys. Guys who talk like that objectify women and they only see women as objects of pleasure, nothing more, nothing less. This is the kind of guy that has multiple women that he is talking to at any given moment or who runs through girls like a stomach flu running through intestines and out the backdoor. Yikes!

In this pool of guys, you will most likely find chronic liars, manipulators and abusers! The moment you sense abusive behavior, whether it be mentally, emotionally or physically, throw him away before you get more invested in him. I want you to understand that you can't change a person's heart. If he was an abuser before you met him, he will be an abuser after you guys start talking. Your beauty, sex, money, cooking, cleaning skills or kind heart cannot change the heart of another human being. Only Jesus can do that. The last thing a guy like that needs is a woman. What he needs is a therapist and he needs it fast. Check out the following statistic that can be found at www.hotline.org

"Over 1 in 3 women (35.6%) and 1 in 4 men (28.5%) in the US have experienced rape, physical violence, and/or stalking by an intimate partner in their lifetime."

The CDC defines an intimate partner as a "current or former partner or spouse." I would further add on that an intimate partner can be anyone you are dating as well. All it takes for someone to be placed in that category is for you both to have consistently exchanged words with each other for any amount of time. The longer you talk to a throw away, the more likely he will introduce you to his abusive behavior.

Potential

This is the category you place a guy in who shows the most promising future. Oxford English Dictionary defines potential as "having or showing the capacity to become or develop into something in the future." The Online Etymology Dictionary says that the root word for potential means power, might or force. If you look very closely at the word potential, you can see that the word potent is the base of it. If you are potent then that means you show a level of strength in something. Basically, what these two word searches tell me is that when someone has potential, it means that they have power or influence in a specific area that is already on display.

For example, when you see a person who is really great at playing the piano, it's safe to say that person has potential to be one of the greatest piano players around. The reason why you can say that is because they are actively pursuing and perfecting their musical craft, enough to catch the eye, or ear, of those around them.

Potential is what you already see a person doing or being, not what you fantasize about a person doing or being. Fantasies are images that we long to become reality. It is where we go to dream, and it gives us things to look forward to, but depending on what part of you creates the images determines if those images are realistic or not.

When it comes to dating, a fantasy is an image you resort to when you don't see it in reality. If it was real, you wouldn't have to fantasize about it.

We have a bad habit of thinking, hoping and dreaming that a guy would become everything that we desire and totally ignore the fact that he is actually nothing like it in reality, not even close. Oftentimes, who we fantasize about and who is in front of us are two different people, and that is a sign for most women that the person you are dating is truly not the person you desire. That is something worth acknowledging. That fantasy you have may be showing you that there might be some things that your soul is starving for to the point where you have to go to a make-believe place just to get it because the person you are dating is not providing it. That's alarming.

One of the most painful things I have watched a woman go through is marrying the wrong guy and suffer from her own choices all because she married her distorted understanding of potential and not the guy's reality. When the honeymoon phase is over, life will sober you up real quick to show you that you picked your fantasy over reality, and that's not what we want to do as young women created on purpose and for a purpose.

"But Brittany, I just know he will be the best guy for me. I can just see it in him."

I have seen things inside people that could have become something great, but they never did. That's because those people never watered the seeds inside themselves. No matter how much "you see" in a person, it is ultimately up to that person to water that seed and make it grow to become visible and tangible. This is why I say only place guys in this category who show actual evidence of the things that would make them a great pick for a life partner. They must be actively watering their own seeds and you must see actual growth of it.

Let me give you some simple examples of someone having potential of something

1. Kind hearted

He should already be displaying kindness to his peers, his family and other people around you, especially yourself.

2. Earning potential

He already shows a drive and determination to provide and take care of his current responsibilities no matter how much he is making at the moment.

3. God seeker

He already has a relationship with God and does not depend on someone to tell him to go and talk to God.

Let me say this and I say it with great care and sobriety; telling a guy to get a better relationship with God will not make him seek God even more. That is a heart posture that he must develop on his own. Marrying him will not change his heart and if he does not desire to know God, he will remain that way until he himself allows Jesus to enter his heart. That decision he makes should never be a decision based on anything you do but simply on how good God is. Place him in the assignment category for now and be willing to care more about his soul than how you would look with him on a "save the date" announcement card. Do not go forward with this guy until there is evidence that God has taken the seat of the throne in his heart.

4. Great leadership

This will already show in his ability to make a decision and execute on it. This will also show in how he interacts with others. Does he care to be an example for others?

If so, how? One huge aspect of great leadership is learning to not follow the crowd, who are really just a bunch of people being led by their feelings and not God's truth. Instead, he chooses to walk down the right path where others will follow him. If he is afraid to be different, then that shows poor leadership skills if any at all. Another sign is that he follows good and healthy examples of manhood who are already mature in the area he wants to grow in. It takes time to develop into a great leader, in fact years, but there must already be evidence to show that he has started the journey.

Potential is always something that's already in a person that has the capacity to grow, not what you hope a person will do or become. So, if a guy does not already have what you are looking for in him, if you cannot see him as a possible spouse and life partner in the state he is in now, then you should not place him in this category. Kindly place him in one of the other 2 categories.

Do not play yourself and try to wait around for a guy, hoping that he will miraculously become what your heart desires. If you do this, you will potentially be setting your heart up for some serious disappointment. Only girls who don't know their worth do this. Remember, you are the prize and it's a man who needs you as a wife, not you who needs him as a husband. He needs your help, you do not need his.

"The Lord God said, 'It is not good for the man to be alone. I will make a helper suitable for him.'" – **Genesis 2:18 (NIV)**

Move forward and keep living your best life, growing and developing into the woman you are destined to be. Make yourself available for someone who does have the necessary things that you desire in a guy. If a previous guy that was not potential develops into potential, only date the new and improved him, IF an opportunity presents itself and IF you really want to. I would definitely be careful in doing this. The choice is yours.

"F" Him!

If you feel like you can't put him in any category just yet, then **F** him! What does the **F** stand for you ask? Exactly what you thought; be friendly toward him until you can figure it out.

Friendly is simply being kind. Nothing more nothing less. Generally, when you first meet a guy or begin to date a guy you are already familiar with, this will be the category you place him in until you intentionally begin to gather data about him. I waited to introduce this category because I don't want this category to be used as a crutch or stalling place. The goal is to place him in A, T or P and that's a decision that you are eventually going to have to make so that you can keep the momentum going.

Notice I said *friendly* and not friends. That's on purpose. I have asked this question so many times; can a girl and a guy truly be friends? I've heard yes and no multiple times but after assessing my own life and talking to other women with "male friends," I have come to this conclusion; it's possible but highly unlikely. Let me break it down for you.

We use the word friend loosely and there are many people we call friends that we should not. A friend is someone that you exchange healthy words with on a consistent basis. They are a person who is physically, emotionally or spiritually available at some capacity and is also able to make a fairly equal exchange with you in those same areas. They are someone you can trust because they have proven themselves to be trustworthy. A friend is simply that, a friend. They have your best interest at heart with no hidden motives. They are a safe person who provides a safe place for you to be vulnerable and to confide in them. That's no surface or light hearted relationship.

When you are dating a guy, you simply don't have the time to develop that level of depth with each other nor should you try to because dating is a short period of time and it does not equal trust, safety and longevity, all the things that a friendship requires. This may sound crazy to you but that's because our culture makes it a practice to get so close so fast and anything that is opposite of that seems crazy.

We want to call everyone a bestie and hubby the first day we meet them when we don't even know their character yet or if they even know how to have good and healthy relationships. Your goal in dating is to not even be friends but to simply gather data. Stop trying to make this deep-felt connection with the guy and just do your job. There will come a time to create a deep connection with him, if the relationship progresses, but not yet. Do investigators try to win victims and suspects over? No, they keep the main thing the main thing so they can solve cases and come to a conclusion. If we adopted this mentality we could eliminate a lot, if not all, heartache, mess and mistakes during the dating phase.

Can a guy and a girl truly be friends? The only way you can be friends with a guy is if there is no possibility of you two ever being together romantically. Don't miss this! The reason why I really believe guys and girls can't simply be friends is because a single guy and a single girl are always open to the possibility of finding a romantic partner, potentially with each other. We are wired this way. If a single guy comes into your life, he knows that it's a possibility that you two can pursue something more than just friends, even if "friendship" was the way he entered your life. Most of the time it's the girl who is completely blind to this while the guy she has been calling "friend" has been secretly liking her for a long time.

Every woman that I have talked to has told me that her single guy friends showed a level of interest in her at some point in their relationship, especially the guys who have been around for years. Do you see what I mean?

So again I say, the only way you can truly be friends with a guy is if there is no possibility of you two ever being together romantically. EVER! The only guys that I can think of who fit into this category are men who are in your family or who play familial roles in your life, and guys that are gay. Straight up! I would like to put men in this category who have authoritative roles in our lives like mentors, coaches, teachers, bosses, etc. but we all know that if they are single then there are possibilities of starting dating relationships with them as well. A woman must be really intune and honest with herself to place a guy like that in a friend category.

There are guys in my life right now who I have placed in the brother category with an iron seal and that will never change. I did that once I realized there was absolutely no possibility of a spark between us, not that I wanted it to be because I was never attracted to any of them in that way, but it really just happened like that. I actually don't look to them as friends at all but more like true brothers in Christ. Once you are a brother you stay there. If I ever talk to them it's like a conversation that a brother and sister have, nothing more nothing less. Could I call them friends? Sure, but I don't communicate with them like a friend would and I truly don't consider them as friends if we go by the definition I laid out.

I say this because I know I have reached a level of maturity to categorize them in this way. Many women have sex with guys they also call their brothers which shows they don't yet have the maturity to have healthy relationships with guys because they don't know how to set proper boundaries and keep them. This is also why I say putting guys in familial categories takes honesty and integrity because dating or having sex with a guy you call a brother shows that you see him as much more than that and you are only deceiving yourself.

Looking back at my relationships, I cringe at the thought of calling the guys in my life friends because at some point, boundary lines were crossed that friends don't cross. I could never talk to them and confide in them like I would a true friend because I knew I couldn't trust them to have my best interest at heart and if given the chance, they would have sex with me, no questions asked. So now, every guy I meet, I am friendly to them until I can place them in a category, even if that category is beyond the dating scope, like the brother category.

When a woman continuously confides in any man that is not her husband, family or trusted authoritative figure, she will begin to develop feelings for him and expect more from him than a friend. That's exactly what I did and if you are honest with yourself, that's what you have done or are doing right now! It's inevitable because we are wired to be attracted to the opposite gender and you cannot undo your God given nature as a woman. This is why you can't just talk to any guy any time you want. There has to be some serious boundaries around that connection.

When you go too deep, beyond the surface, with a guy in conversation you will begin to expect him to give you a return on that investment. You will begin to expect your emotions to be cared for and to be matched. The truth is, you will begin to expect a husband's response from him and he is not your husband. This is so dangerous to a young woman's heart and it's actually self-inflicted emotional abuse because you are using that relationship in a wrong way. You are mishandling your wiring as a woman.

For more on how deep the conversation should go with a guy you are dating, purchase my book, 35 *Tips on How to Win at Dating.*

The Phases of Dating

There are three phases of dating that I believe are necessary if you want to date with any level of intention and not get stuck anywhere, and these phases start in pre-dating as you are putting the A.T.P dating method to work. These phases are in no way meant for you to go through alone. Dating is a collective approach and it's wise if you make sure your father, family and wise circle are heavily involved.

This is not a linear model, meaning you don't have to apply them in this exact order. You may go from phase one, to three then two. You may go through all three phases after one conversation with a guy, in fact, I encourage that. I list these phases in this order for readability and clarity sake but use them as you see fit. Let's briefly talk about them.

Phase 1: Gather Data

As we have already been discussing, get as much info about the guy and record it. This phase really starts the moment you engage with him with an interest to move forward. The best way to record data is to write it down. It's one thing to hear something about someone and it's another thing to see it on paper. This is for your own good because when thoughts or information is stuck in your head, they have the potential of being tweaked, manipulated or flat out changed to something that it is not. Who would do that to the information in your head you ask? You! Any unhealed part of your soul will more than likely try to talk you into giving a bright, red flag a green pass.

For example, you may meet a guy and learn that he has a child but is not in the child's life. He may give a really good-sounding reason as to why that is. His reason may be that the mother of the child is hostile and manipulative and prevents him from seeing his child. To you, that may sound like a legit reason for him to be absent from his child's life. You may see the hurt, or disgust on his face when talking about it, which will sway you even more to side with him and his decision to stay away.

But when you write that information down and see it for what it is, you will notice that a bad attitude from the mother is not a legit reason for him to be an absent father. That's a huge, HUGE, character flaw and a sign of immaturity on his end. If he is treating his child this way, then he is showing you that he has the potential to treat any future kids the same way, potential kids he may have with you if you choose to go forward with him.

When writing this info down, you will be giving yourself a chance to see this crucial information about him without any other influences to sway your decision-making, like his cute face, choice of incriminating words, tone or facial expressions.

Gathering data should also never be solely left up to you. Allow this person to meet your wise circle so they can have conversations with him as well. Never date alone, I repeat, NEVER date alone. Your circle will be able to pick up on things as well and add to the conversation you have about this person as you assess him. This brings me to the next dating phase.

Phase 2: Assess the Data

After you get that data, it's up to you to do something with it. This is where women get stuck, and I mean stuck, stuck. This is why you see women become long-term girlfriends and stay girls (not maturing into womanhood) because they don't know what to do with the information they have gathered about the guy. This allows him to keep her from growing into a woman with more productivity, like a wife. For most young women, they were never intentional about gathering data to begin with, let alone assessing it.

How do you assess the information you have learned about a guy? You do that by comparing the information to the highest standard there is, the Word of God.

You must assess where this guy is in relation to how God created a young man to operate in this world. This is crucial because if you continue with a guy who is not actively maturing into manhood and advancing in his relationship with God, then that will be one of the biggest dating mistakes you make as a young woman. He will usher you onto a path of disobedience, delay and despair (the triple D effect), and that's a road that is most traveled, yet most destructive. Any guy you connect with must first be connected to the source, God. Only then will he be open to hearing God as He tells him how to treat you, pursue you and lead you if this dating relationship were to advance forward.

Don't let this phase intimidate you. Begin to compare him to the truths of God that you already know. If God is kind, is he? If God is loving, is he? If God is productive, forgiving, integrous, is he? In no way am I saying this is a check box kind of assessment, but it's a great start. A guy may seem like he has all the qualities that reflect God but you still may end up feeling like something is off. That's called discernment. To get more discernment, you must allow the Holy Spirit, the spirit of discernment, into your life. You need to always date with the Holy Spirit and heavily depend on Him, not only in dating but in life in general. If you don't know the Holy Spirit, I will make sure you do by time this girl chat is over.

"When the Spirit of truth comes, he will guide you into all the truth…" – **John 16:13 (ESV)**

If you feel ill-equipped to make this kind of comparison, it may mean you have more learning to do before you step into the dating world, and that's a wonderful assessment of yourself. High five girl! Give yourself a chance to grow your love for God and discernment for guys by reading the Holy Bible. Some starting points are Genesis chapters 1-3, 1 Corinthians chapter 13, Galatians chapter 5, Ephesians chapter 5, and 1 John, 2 John and 3 John.

Another great resource to help you make this assessment is a book called, *"Male Vs. Man, How to Honor Women, Teach Children and Elevate Men to Change the World,"* by Dondre Whitfield. This book not only teaches guys how to be men, but it trains women how to tell the difference between a boy in a man's body, and a man who has assumed the responsibility of manhood and who is ready to pursue a woman to marry. It's a must-read!

This part of dating is huge and can be overwhelming to anyone's heart. Again, in no way should you do it alone. This is why it's necessary that you have a squad of wise people surrounding you as well as a wise father figure helping you assess the data you have gathered. This leads me to the next phase.

Phase 3: Share the Data

Once you have made assessments or at least attempted to, you must share what you have discovered. I can't stress this phase enough. I learned the hard way that if you date in isolation, you will more than likely date wrong. I see it all the time. The heart of the woman needs to be protected at all times and a huge part of that is exposing every person who is trying to win it over. There is no way that you as a woman can make a huge decision, like potentially choosing a guy that you will marry, all on your own. You are a limited human being, and this is not the time to be prideful or independent.

One thing that all guys are good at is talking, and I don't mean saying a lot of words but saying the "right" words. By right words, I mean words to get you to do what they want you to do or give them what they want you to give them.

These are words that will lock you in and keep you stuck on him. Have you ever had a friend just fall (there's that word fall again) head over heels for a guy, and it seemed like during that fall she busted her head wide open, spilling out all common sense, good judgment and self-respect? Seriously, it happens to the best of us. You start to see her do silly girl stuff, things that she said she would never do.

"Girl, he's not moving in with me."

Three weeks later, you show up to her house and see ole dude laid up on the couch playing video games. What happened? I will tell you. He got into her head and told her something that his actions didn't. He told her a lie and she believed it.

In the Bible, there is a man named Paul who was once a murderer before Jesus changed his entire life. He was heavily deceived, thinking that what he was doing was right, so he has much authority to speak on the topic of deception. He traveled to a place called Galatia to preach to the people about Jesus being crucified and the way to God, which is through faith in Jesus. After that encounter with the people, he later learned that they no longer believed how he taught them. They began to believe that the way to God was through works instead of faith. He asked them this one question.

"You foolish Galatians! Who has bewitched you? Before your very eyes Jesus Christ was clearly portrayed as crucified." – **Galatians 3:1 (NIV)**

I would ask that young woman the same question, "Who has bewitched you?"

Bewitched means to have a spell cast over you. And it's not what you think. This ain't no hocus pocus mess but this is real-life stuff that goes down every day all day right before your very ears.

A spell is a lie told to you that binds your will. It is words spoken to you that you believe, key word *believe*, and those words control what you do.

For example, if some guy tells you that he will never leave you, that he loves you and you believe it without allowing his words to be put to the test, you have been bewitched. He has cast his spell on you and it worked! Well, how can you tell if what he says is true or a lie? Simple, by examining his actions and the authority or lack of authority he has to even say what he is saying to you. If he does not have the heart of God for you, then he doesn't love you because no one can truly love you without the presence of God to do that. God is love, and without God, there is no love.

"So, we have come to know and to believe the love that God has for us. God is love, and whoever abides in love abides in God, and God abides in him." – **1 John 4:16 (ESV)**

If he says he will never leave you, and he is not married to you, he does not have the authority to say those words to you and mean it. Only the one who is actually committed to you can say those words to you. His action of marrying you is him telling you that he won't walk away from you. Any words spoken about it but not being about it are words full of hot air. Meaningless!

Have you ever heard a young woman say, "I want to leave him, but every time I try, I go right back to him." It's because her will has been bound, and she has been trapped by his words or his spell. How was it cast? Through sex.

The act of sex is actually words a man speaks to the deepest part of your soul without him ever saying anything with his mouth. Through sex, he tells you he is committed to you, that he will protect you and never leave you, but just like the previous example, if he is not married to you when he had sex with you, then it's yet another lie. And get this, marriage does not make a lie true all of a sudden. You can't turn lies into truth; you have to repent from lies and change the lying heart. If he were to marry you, he would only lie about something else because lying is a part of who he is.

When it comes to illegal sex, you're not aware of the spell cast on you but your soul is. It shows by your inability to walk away from the guy as you desperately look to him to make good on that empty promise he made to you. It truly is the best way to trap a young woman and the enemy knows it. He got me this way.

> **When it comes to illegal sex, you're not aware of the spell cast on you but your soul is.**
>
> #TheGirlfriendTrap

This is why you can't afford to make dating decisions in isolation because you can very well choose to be with someone you should have never said hello to and get caught up in a spell. How about this, you can still get caught up in a spell with a guy who just might be for you but because lies entered in through sex, the effects of it will still be the same. You will still need the power of Jesus to sober you up and keep you sober or that toxic potion you sipped on will be preserved, waiting on your kids to be the next victims. (The enemy will make sure your kids fall to the same deceit which is a generational curse that you passed on to them because of your own actions)

Had someone else known about this relationship and the kind of words that were being spoken between you two, they could have identified the trap and saved you from it if you were willing to be saved.

The truth is, there should be no privacy about your life when it comes to your trusted squad because you need to be able to expose your weak flesh at any moment. If you feel the need to hide anything, more than likely, it's because it's something unhealthy that your flesh wants but is not good for your spirit. You will need help to overcome it and to get that you need all eyes and ears on deck. Don't be your own worst enemy, the devil has already taken that role in your life.

Phase 4: Make a Decision

As you get the data, assess the data, share the data and put it all on repeat, this should help you make a decision. That decision is one of 2 choices: continue to date this person another day or call it quits. Simple as that. If you come across any information that is incompatible with your body, soul or spirit, you must be willing to make the decision to end the dating relationship.

I want you to know that you not only have the choice to make this decision, but you have the responsibility to. Why? Because you have the ability to respond to a decision like this. You have the God-given power and will to say yes or no to anyone and mean it. Never allow someone into your life that tries to make you feel otherwise. If the guy you are dating is a person like that, that's even more reason to walk away from him quick, fast and in a hurry. Anyone who does not take no for an answer has some serious boundary and respect issues and there is no telling what that person is capable of doing or how far they are willing to step over your boundaries. That's a dangerous person, and your squad should know about this if they have not already picked up on it!

This is another reason why a young woman should date with her father. A father's voice is authoritative and carries more weight than hers and if need be, consequences. A father helps his daughter use her voice, and in many cases, step in on her behalf. The reason why women are the most battered gender when it comes to dating is because the father's voice has been absent and does not speak on her behalf when she needs it the most.

After collaborative assessments and considerations, if you feel confident to continue to date this individual, then keep the phases in heavy rotation. Eventually, the goal is to move toward marriage. But the decision to call it quits is always on the table before ever reaching the point of commitment, and you should be willing to make it if need be, with no shame or guilt.

CHAPTER 14

The Courting Relationship

*"Look carefully then how you walk, not as unwise but as wise, making the best use of the time, because the days are evil." – **Ephesians 5:15-16 (ESV)***

Since I got out of the girlfriend trap, God has shown me so much about the importance of self-esteem and how a young woman's heart should always be protected. He has shown me the power of His love and guidance and it's simply unmatched, hands down. God is all knowing. He knows the end of things before it ever begins. It would be foolish of me to not allow Him to cover me, instruct me, lead and guide me through life, especially when it comes to guys.

God has also blessed me with a brother-in-law that is one of the wisest men I know. I love my father, but I was never afforded the spiritual, emotional and physical safety that dads provide. I know many of you share my same story. God allowed my brother-in-law to become the fatherly voice that I never had on earth and has given me all of that through him. I go to him for everything. I trust his character and his heart for me and because of that, I will never date without him as long as he is alive to help me. It would be foolish of me to have full access to the wisdom that God gives him and not take full advantage of it.

This is why I stress the importance of dating under the covering of a father, whether it be a real one, father figure, or a father's voice from somewhere else, because I know the safety you experience first-hand. Even before my brother fully stepped into that role, all I had was Father God and He is the ultimate covering and fatherly voice that every woman needs, I mean EVERY woman. He was and still is enough. But let me say this, because of his design of family and structure, he made sure that I had a tangible male presence in my life to model His love, direction and protection for me. When you surrender to Father God and get in order, He will provide for you everything that you need in its proper time.

Initially, God took me completely off the dating scene and started me on another level of learning and healing. He then placed my brother in my life full time. He used, and still uses, my brother's voice as a reinforcement to what He was already telling me. I just had to listen. I wanted to share that because even if you don't have a father figure as tangible as I explained, you have Father God right here and right now and I need you to understand how powerful that is. It's Father God's voice that you need above all other voices and He gives that to every person freely if you open your heart to Him and read His words in the Holy Bible. It's all about doing what He says and if you don't listen to His word then you won't listen to an earthly father figure when he appoints one to you no matter how good or right he is.

God the father and the father figure in my life have completely transformed how I see relationships and it has even changed how I allow a young man to pursue me and I'm going to share a bit with you right now.

The only man that I will ever allow to pursue me has to, one, know what he wants. He must have some clarity concerning his life and future. Two, he has to be marriage focused. He needs to show interest in me with the intent of marriage. I will never again in my God given life entertain a man who has a nonchalant approach to commitment, with words like, "I don't want to get married," "it's just a piece of paper," "let's just go with the flow," or, "I want to get married but not right now." I can tell you that a lot of your heartache is because you have entertained someone like that and it's a waste of your precious time. Third, he has to see my value as a woman and approach me with the utmost respect.

These are the bare minimum requirements he must meet to even pursue me, and I encourage you to take on this same attitude towards guys. With that being said, when it comes to my life, this is how the courting process will start with a guy. If a guy is serious about pursuing me, I will direct him to my brother (father figure). After my brother talks to him and gathers information about him, however many convos that takes, if he decides that he has good intentions and is marriage potential for me, then he will give him the green light to pursue me to begin a courting relationship. As we court and information continues to be gathered, if my brother ultimately concludes that he is not a good fit for me, guess what? That courting relationship will end. I trust his judgement enough to see things, even if I don't see them at that time.

At some point, if you have been dating a guy, the conversation needs to turn to marriage in a more focused manner because that is the whole purpose of dating for a purpose driven woman.

#TheGirlfriendTrap

If he is not pursuing you for marriage then he is pursuing you for sex.

#TheGirlfriendTrap

What does that look like? It looks like having a real and honest conversation with each other, knowing each other's true intentions for pursuing each other and bringing an authoritative father figure upon the scene if that has not already happened. This kind of move puts this dating relationship to the ultimate test, setting it ablaze to burn out any impurities or wrong motives that were hidden or you just didn't know were there. If he crumbles underneath the pressure, then he was never marriage material to start with because if he can't stand to face a man made of flesh then he won't stand a chance in face of Father God who will summon him to give an account concerning you one way or another.

Any guy who shows interest in me, and I in him, will be entering into a courting relationship and that will be the definition of our interaction with one another. Why else would I allow a guy to pursue me? You need to ask yourself the same question. If he is not pursuing you for marriage then he is pursuing you for sex. Straight up! A guy who is intentional will not make you dig for answers and if that's the case, I would definitely lean even more on your father/squad of wisdom to reinforce the need for accountability or let him go.

How to Court

Maintaining a neutral environment during the courting relationship is key. You want to be able to always think clearly and judge the fruits of his life with wisdom and discernment. You don't want to put any unhealthy expectations on him nor assume anything. How do you keep a clear and sober mind throughout this entire process? You have to maintain your boundaries. Here are a few life saving tips that will keep this process healthy and purposeful:

1. **Stay Intentional** – Because courting is intentional, you both want to be on the same page and stay on the same page. If marriage is not the goal then there is no point in courting. If you both lose focus, you both will begin to drift. What will happen is, as you talk to him more and get to know him on a deeper level, you will create a bond with him that will only get stronger with words, touch and expectation. This will awaken your desires to give more of yourself to him and function as a wife with no legal grounds to actually express those desires. This is self-inflicted abuse upon your heart and will lead to sin and disappointment. Stay focused!

2. **Leave Him How You Found Him** – As you begin to interact with a guy and get to know him, you have to realize that he is not yours until you sign a marriage license and say, "I do." This means that you can't do whatever you want with him and until he is yours he is potentially someone else's spouse.

   > God loves him just as much as he loves you and He doesn't want his heart to be tainted or hurt in any kind of way. The same goes for your heart. You have to develop a **"Hands off"** mentality. You don't kiss him, have sex with him, move in with him or take him on as your own in any way. If you do, you are tainting someone else's spouse, causing him to cheat on his future wife, even if his future wife is you! Think about that for a moment. When someone takes something that's not theirs or walks onto a land without permission from the owner, it's called stealing and trespassing and until he goes to your father (natural and/or spiritual) to ask to have you for a lifetime, he has no right to you and you have no right to him. Don't be an accomplice to a crime.

3. **No Alone Time** – In order to leave him how you found him the best way to do that is to never find yourself alone with him. I know, I know! You're grown, you can do whatever you want to do, right? Wrong! *Humility always looks better on you than pride.* Finding yourself alone with the opposite sex is the biggest trap you can set for yourself. It opens the door for temptation to come in and make you forget all about boundaries and why you set them in the first place. Ask anyone who has failed to honor God with their body how it happened. They were alone! For more on why this is a no no, go back to bait #2's how to let go of the bait.

4. **Lead with Accountability** – Be open and transparent with those around you that you trust concerning this courting process. This will keep you honest to yourself, the guy, and to God. If you feel like you are going to have to lie or hide what you are doing or saying to the guy then that's a good sign that you don't need to be doing or saying it at all. This will also keep you guys from wasting time or prolonging the process. Tell me, why does anyone need to court for years to figure out if someone is right for them? That makes no sense and shows a lack of intention and confusion, two things you should run from. Give yourself a timetable to help you be intentional. <u>In my honest opinion</u>, even 1 year is too long to make a decision. Anything past that is alarming!

This is all to protect him and yourself from the evil one (the devil), which is the true way to express your love to someone. If at any time you guys find out that you are not compatible with one another, you can walk away as healthy and free as you came. This means no physical connections, no deep heart connections, no baggage transferred, no naked pictures shared, no children to fight over, no STDs transferred, no "I hate you's" because you broke my heart, no tainted memories you wish you never had and no having to pack up and move out. You will still have your integrity, moral excellence and witness intact.

One of the things that I regret as a girlfriend was destroying my witness and integrity as a young woman who professed to know and live for God. Because I had sex with him and crossed so many boundary lines, I made my walk with Christ out to be mocked, exposed to gossip and ridicule and I just didn't set the best example for those who looked up to me.

I was also a willing party to his spiritual brokenness with God and that is something I felt horrible about. This very thing caused me to repent before him as well as apologize to him, and God of course. When you truly love someone, you will want the best for them even if that means you walking away from him for good and you guys never becoming one in marriage. The beauty of walking away without physical contact is that you actually build his faith in God and his trust in women. You prove to him that there are women who exist that are not ashamed to be different from the rest, by respecting sex and its proper place of marriage and respecting the human body as well. It gives him hope. It shows him what to look for in a wife and it even equips him on how to teach his future daughters to walk in integrity. How you interact with him matters big time and will leave a lasting impression on his very soul. Let it be an impression that heaven applauds.

> **66** #TheGirlfriendTrap
>
> *The beauty of walking away without physical contact is that you actually build his faith in God and his trust in women.*
>
> #TheGirlfriendTrap **99**

Your Role in All of This

So, what does this mean for you? Throughout this entire process what is your title? Remember the question I proposed to you earlier? Let's finally get back to it. Sorry I made you wait but it was for good reason.

"If I'm not a girlfriend and I'm called to be a wife, then what am I in between time?"

The answer is... **you!** You are simply you! Your role in all of this is to be your God given self, nothing more nothing less and your title is the name God gave you.

I know you were probably waiting for me to drop this big mysterious title on you as to what you are to a guy during this courting relationship. But there is more to your name and simply being "you" than you think.

I wrote this girl chat to show ladies like you that it's crucial to believe more about yourself and to raise your standards. You are called to be and function as something so much greater than what society has subjected you to.

#TheGirlfriendTrap

Whatever you are now is more real and valid than any illegitimate title you label yourself in an illegitimate boyfriend-girlfriend relationship.

#TheGirlfriendTrap

When I say your role is to be you, I mean you are to be free, living your best life as an image bearer of God in Heaven with no stress or pressure to be anything or anyone else. It's so important for you to know the power of your existence as a young woman right now because whatever you are now is more real and valid than any illegitimate title you label yourself in an illegitimate boyfriend-girlfriend relationship.

What does "being you" look like?

It looks like being:

1. A woman
2. A daughter
3. A student
4. A friend
5. An athlete
6. A dancer
7. A businesswoman
8. An author
9. An auntie
10. A sister
11. A mother
12. A speaker
13. A mentor
14. An encourager
15. A chef
16. An entrepreneur
17. A prayer warrior
18. A creator

19. An Influencer
20. A Worshiper
21. A _____ (fill in the blank)

I mean, pick one! There are so many to choose from and this list only touches the endless things you can currently operate in with legality, dignity and respect. Being "you" includes so many things and the most important "you" that you should strive to be is a young woman that pursues a committed relationship with God.

Let me give you some defining language to this whole courting process. What are you to him? You are nothing more to him than a potential spouse. He should simply see you as a young woman, created by God and deserving the utmost respect. And you must make that known to him. Boundaries!

So, when people ask you, "are you guys together? Are you guys boyfriend and girlfriend?" Your response could be, "no, we are not together, we are courting. I am getting to know him to see if we are marriage compatible." This kind of response will open a door for conversation to talk about dating with purpose, and even help others expand their mind in their own dating life.

CHAPTER 15

The Proposal—Will You Say Yes?

Dating with purpose opens your life up to another level of maturity, discernment and peace, all coming from God who desires you to have it even more. But it doesn't start with having the right guy. Before you ever thought about being with a man that you can spend the rest of your life with, God thought about spending this life and eternity with you. He loves you so much, more than you will ever be able to comprehend, and He wants to know you on an intimate level. Although this book is about relationships and dating, no relationship will ever be fruitful without first entering into a relationship with the one who loves you to no end.

Your Forever Love

I have talked about God and His design for relationships, but I can't assume that every queen that is engaging with me during this girl chat has a personal relationship with Him. Allow me to ask you this question: Do you know the Lord God for yourself? Do you believe in Him? Do you believe Him to be your creator and the greatest lover ever known to mankind?

Do you want to know why I believe and have faith in Him? Here is just one reason; because our very existence proves that He exists and that He is God to all mankind. You don't believe me? Go look into the mirror, tell me if you don't see traces of His divine power all over you. Or go outside and look up or down. Do you really think the green hues and the sky blues came to be on its own? You have so many interactions and run-ins with these complex creations that they have become so common to you, so common that you miss the simple message God speaks to you though them day in and day out: "Here I am, I am yours and you are mine." Sometimes, God seems huge and so complex that our brains fail to understand Him. We seem so small in comparison to Him, yet He wants to be with us, with you. How do I know? Because of the love he showed to prove it.

"For God so loved the world that he gave his one and only Son, that whoever believes in him shall not perish but have eternal life. For God did not send his Son into the world to condemn the world, but to save the world through him. Whoever believes in him is not condemned, but whoever does not believe stands condemned already because they have not believed in the name of God's one and only Son. This is the verdict: Light has come into the world, but people loved darkness instead of light because their deeds were evil. Everyone who does evil hates the light, and will not come into the light for fear that their deeds will be exposed. But whoever lives by the truth comes into the light, so that it may be seen plainly that what they have done has been done in the sight of God." – **John 3:16-21 (NIV)**

I remember wanting love from a guy so bad that I overlooked the love that gives me breath to live every day. I overlooked God's presence and all the good things He wants for me, like contentment in my skin and status as a single woman, emotional wholeness and His purpose for me. He showed me my worth in Him and how He spent his very life, through Jesus Christ, just to have me forever. Talk about expensive! He told me why he put me here on this earth, which is to make Him known to others around me. He wants to tell you the truth of who you are too. Your highest

#TheGirlfriendTrap

Your highest calling is not a relationship with a guy, a career, or a certain status, but it's intimacy with God.

#TheGirlfriendTrap

calling is not a relationship with a guy, a career, or a certain status, but it's intimacy with God.

In that intimacy, in-to-me-see, with God, you will develop a stance of contentment. Contentment is the heart posture to have if you want to live a healthy and fulfilling life, no matter what your relationship status is. It can only come through an understanding of God through Christ. Rehearse your satisfaction with what you already have, the love and friendships you already have and the love of a father that God provides. I encourage you to start engaging with God and let him show you what true commitment and emotional health looks like. He cares deeply about your well-being and is committed to you living in the abundance of His pleasures. He will show you your identity and the truth of who you really are, which every young woman should know before she ever tries to get to know a guy.

"Before I formed you in the womb I knew you..." – **God, Jeremiah 1:5 (NIV)**

Let's have a moment of truth. Are you even ready to be pursued by a guy right now? The truth is, most young women who are reading this are not ready to date and be pursued for marriage right now and that is absolutely okay. Here are some signs that you may not be ready.

1. You are in a relationship with a guy looking to him to heal and validate you (to confirm who you are).
2. You just got out of a relationship and have not identified why you were there, the wrong turns you made, and the right turns you need to make going forward.
3. You are using sex as a way to get a guy, medicate pain or emotional distress.
4. You don't know God yet which means you don't know yourself or where you are even going in life.
5. You are not willing to be humble and honest with yourself about your current heart condition.
6. You are not content with being single and pursuing self-healing.
7. You don't know what it means to be a wife or what womanhood looks like.

    ***Healthy tip: Find a healthy, God-filled married woman to learn from.

8. You have not lived life yet to even know what you want in life. (This includes all teenagers and most 18 and 19 year olds. Legal age does not mean you are grown and ready. You need to mature. If you rush to date and to marry more than likely you will be rushing to divorce.)

If you just came to the conclusion that you are not ready, then you are in an amazing place. Living in truth and authenticity marks the beginning of true change and building a life that will be solid and fruitful. Truth is the only foundation to build anything on.

I came to that conclusion in my early twenties and I have been completely guy free for almost 8 years now, healing, learning and transforming into the woman God has always created me to be. It has been the BEST time of my life and that's an understatement. I have been learning who I really am and how to trust God with my life, something I was too afraid to do while in a relationship with a guy. I never knew I could be this content. With a heart at peace, I look forward to all that God has planned for me, whether I am single or married.

*"I know the plans I have for you, plans to prosper you and not harm you, plans to give you hope and a future" – **God,** Jeremiah 29:11 (NIV)*

Queen, a relationship with God was, is and will always be the highest goal of life and if you desire marriage, that marriage will be to prepare you for your first and true love, Jesus. It always points back to Him. Trust Him with your heart.

"The strongest women I know are those who have taken time away from men to get closer to God" – Chris Davis, married 15 years

Whether you know it or not, you are in the sight of the Lord God and with His love shown to you through His Son Jesus, he has asked you to be one with Him. He has asked you to be in a loving committed relationship with Him where He will forever be yours and you will forever be His. He declares and reassures people of their salvation who believe in Jesus as their Lord and Savior and confess it with their mouth.

"If you declare with your mouth, 'Jesus is Lord,' and believe in your heart that God raised him from the dead, you will be saved. For it is with your heart that you believe and are justified, and it is with your mouth that you profess your faith and are saved." – **Romans 10:9-10**

In the Bible, not only is God depicted as a father, but He embodies His love and commitment through His Son Jesus Christ to a people who believe in Him, the Church. Jesus is referred to as the groom to the Church and the Church is referred to as the bride of Jesus, who is also called the sacrificial Lamb.

"Let us rejoice and be glad and give the glory to Him, for the marriage of the Lamb has come and His bride has made herself ready." – **Revelation 19:7**

God has popped the question! He has asked you to be in a committed relationship with Him. Will you prepare your heart for Him and become a part of His Church, the bride? Will you say yes?

Allow me to pray for you:

"Lord, I thank you for the beautiful soul who is reading this right now. It's not by coincidence that you brought her here. Continue to show her the value you placed on her beyond these pages as she decides which way to go with her dating life and where she stands with you. You have called her to live the highest life she can possibly live, a life grounded in you. I pray that she will no longer see herself as anything less than what you created her to be. Change how she sees you and how she sees herself. In Jesus name"

To say yes to The Lord God means you are saying no to all other false wannabe gods. If you have said yes and have decided to be committed to God and a covered woman from this day forward then take a conscious moment to repent and turn away from your sin, from everyone and everything you have made a false god in your life. Put your hope in Jesus Christ to save you from the penalty of your sins and to set you in right standing with Father God.

"Now when they heard this they were cut to the heart, and said to Peter and the rest of the apostles, 'Brothers, what shall we do?' And Peter said to them, 'Repent and be baptized every one of you in the name of Jesus Christ for the forgiveness of your sins, <u>and you will receive the gift of the Holy Spirit</u>.'" – **Acts 2:37-38 (ESV)**

Repeat this prayer out loud.

"Lord God, I thank you for loving me. I thank you for keeping me alive to experience this very moment. I admit that I have neglected you as my God, father and the lover of my soul. I admit that I have sinned against you, but now, I want a fully committed relationship with you. God, I turn from every imposter, false god, every idol and fake covering, and I turn to you with open arms and an accepting heart.

I confess your son Jesus as Lord of my life and I believe that you sent Him to earth as a sacrificial lamb to die in my place and save me from my sins. I believe that He rose on the third day with all power and authority in heaven and on earth and that He now sits at the right hand of You, interceding for me every day. With this confession I profess my commitment to you with the love you freely give me, and I ask that you cover me from this day forward. With joy, I receive the amazing gift of The Holy Spirit that only you can give. In Jesus name...amen!

The Decision

If you just committed your life to God by repenting and believing in His Son Jesus Christ, then you have made the absolute best decision you could ever make. May your life begin to bear fruit to show proof of your decision.

"Produce fruit in keeping with repentance." – **Matthew 3:8 (NIV)**

This decision has just officially made you a committed woman. And this same decision now opens the door for you to make many more that are great in nature. The next one is choosing to no longer be a girlfriend and instead rise to your calling as a wife, a committed woman on earth.

For a person's mindset to change and honor God is not only a blessing but a miracle from above. Choosing to be a wife, not a girlfriend, is one of the best decisions you can make when it comes to relationships and the health of your heart. But making your mind up is the first step. Now it's time to walk it out.

Because lack of commitment is the cultural norm, you're going to be challenged in this area, especially by boyfriends. You may have people look at you crazy, even those around you who have always known you to be one way and enjoy the version of you that stays on ground level with them. That's okay! People who don't believe they can rise to anything greater than where they are will always pressure you to stay and conform to the status quo. But you are different. You are completely unique and conforming to what everyone else is doing is so overrated and an insult to yourself. Instead, allow yourself to transform into a brand new young woman with a renewed heart and mind, one that will no longer accept anything less than what God has declared for you.

Let's keep it 100! It's scary, dang near terrifying, to step into something new when you have lived one way for so long. Whether it be a new location, a new job or a new mindset, it takes time to get used to, but it's worth it. As I continue to live my life, I am learning that it is impossible to go to the next step without first taking your foot off the previous step. This may mean you leaving some things behind. You may have to leave some current habits that you have, some places that you normally attend, some friends and even family that have been around for years and yes, even a boyfriend that you currently have. I know! Just reading that may make you feel like your heart is about to shatter into pieces. I felt the same way.

The thought of letting go of my then boyfriend prevented me from truly letting go because I didn't want to go through the grief of losing someone "so close to me." This is when God began to change my perspective about letting go. **It's not a loss, it's an exchange.** God wanted to give me the things I had been looking for my entire life but as long as I was holding on to my little false version of love, comfort and validation, He wasn't able to give me the real thing. If God is calling you to a new position, it's because he has something better for you.

#TheGirlfriendTrap

It's not a loss, it's an exchange.

#TheGirlfriendTrap

If He is telling you to let some friends go, it's because He has new knowledge that He wants to give to you and eventually new people that He wants to bring into your life. These people will help push you into clarity and purpose. If He is calling you to let go of a boyfriend, queen, it's because he wants to give you commitment, even if that commitment is found with the same guy. Let go of him as a boyfriend so that God can give him to you as a husband, IF you both have turned from your own sins and turned to God individually, and IF it is in line with God's word and really, IF it is in His will for your life. You will never move forward in life without first trusting in the One who knows your future. And even if God says that guy is not the right one for you, trust that He is preparing a person who is not only better for you but godly for you.

#TheGirlfriendTrap

What I am reaching for is greater than what I'm leaving behind.

#TheGirlfriendTrap

This is my new life motto that He gave me when I struggled to let go of my then boyfriend of 4 years: **What I am reaching for is greater than what I'm leaving behind.** It has yet to be a lie.

When I asked God if my then boyfriend was for me, the final answer was...no! Although it hurt, I accepted it with much pain but no hesitation because I knew He would heal me and bless me with his best. He has not failed me yet and I know He never will.

You have been having this girlfriend talk with me, now it's time to have this talk with the guy you have been talking to. Let me help you.

CHAPTER 16

The Talk

Before having this talk, remember the decision you made to no longer be a girlfriend but a wife. Keep in my mind why you made this decision to help keep you focused so you won't fall back into the old mindset that you had before, no matter his response.

This can be tough, especially if you feel very deeply for this person, but remember that God has a purpose for you and you can no longer waste time living beneath that purpose. Changing your mind means changing your relationship status. You don't have to find strength in yourself to do this. God will supply that for you.

"I lift up my eyes to the hills. From where does my help come? My help comes from the Lord, who made heaven and earth" – **Psalm 121:1-2 (NIV)**

Questions

Dating with purpose is a standard that should always be made clear from the very beginning. You might not have known to create that standard before, but you know now and it's not too late. So, let's get back to the basics. Start by asking the guy these questions.

1. What does dating mean to you?
2. Why are you talking to me?
3. What amount of time is the longest relationship you have ever been in? Why?
4. What are your thoughts on marriage?

Don't show your hand, initially, by telling him that you want commitment. Your goal is to get as much information as possible. Make it a natural conversation. It's not an interview or a checklist that you are working through, so you want to go easy and feed in your questions as it moves along, even if the convo lasts for a few days. This will help him feel relaxed and when someone feels comfortable, they feel comfortable enough to tell the truth. If he feels like he is being interviewed, he will begin to manufacture the best answers to tell you what he thinks you want to hear. You know how job interviews go. Even a great guy will try to give his best answers to keep you around.

Responses

Depending on how he responds to these few questions will let you know where he stands with you and ultimately where you stand with him.

1. **"I Don't want to be married"**: This lets you know that he has no purpose with you and you will always be a girlfriend if you stay with him. He is content with playing house as long as you are.

2. **"I want to be married but not right now...eventually"**: This is a tricky response because it puts you in a gray area, making you feel conflicted about how to respond. Let me add some clarity.

> Remember, the point of dating is to marry! Period! If he is not ready or in a position to marry, then he should not be dating. That leads you on. It's like turning the stove on and putting all the ingredients into a pot to make a dish but then saying, "I'm not ready to make it just yet," sitting the pot on the counter. The fire will still burn (which is dangerous) and the food will start to rot and stink as it sits there...waiting.

> If you say "okay" within your heart and stay his girlfriend, you just taught him how to treat you and more than likely, things will go right back to how they were. Please, understand this, not calling yourself his girlfriend but still acting like you are is you missing the entire conversation we just had in this book. There needs to be a complete

change in how you act and interact with this guy and every guy you encounter from here on out.

If you break it off with him, he will either prepare himself for marriage because he wants to have you as his wife or he will continue to stay in limbo, possibly finding another girl to "not be ready" with. Either way, you have to take yourself out of the equation for him to figure out what he is doing with his life. Trust me, I know how challenging that is to do. But by doing this, you teach him your value and what you believe you are worth. You have to teach him how to treat you and if you don't, no one else will!

P.S. Look at this as a win win! Whichever way it goes, you are on the path to becoming a wife and having a purposeful relationship because if he does not prepare to marry, then he's making room for the guy who will come into your life READY to commit to you. OKAY!!!

3. **"My intentions are to Marry"**: This answer keeps him in the running as a potential husband, opening himself up to be asked more questions, many more questions. At this point it's a must that you bring your father figure and or wise circle upon the scene and quickly! You need help to continue on with this process and to make sure that this dude is not just saying what you want to hear…because these kinds of guys run rampant and they are out there! Peep game! His actions will always reveal what's really in his heart.

More questions would be:

1. Do you believe in God/Jesus?

> This is actually the 1st question to ask before dating. If he is not a believer then it doesn't matter if he wants to marry you or not. He is not the one! Disbelief in God is an incompatibility that will always birth instability no matter how good of a guy he may be.

2. What are your views on kids?
3. What are your views on money?
4. What are your views on sex?

5. What are your life/career goals?

If I were to list all possible questions to ask him, this book would go on and on. By asking him these questions you are now doing what you should have done initially, which is to gather data. As you ask these questions, a great way to do that is around your father/ trusted circle so that what is said can be investigated (not with bad intention but for clarity) and with other wise people around, it will open your conversations up and reveal even more insight. Incorporate the dating phases and method until you come to a decision to move forward with him or move on from him.

For more questions to ask a potential spouse, I strongly recommend getting the book, *Before the Next Step: Questions Before "I Do,"* by Carrington and Ashley Brown on Amazon. It has over 300 questions to ask the both of you...WOW!

This is your chance to start over but doing it in a healthy way with love and accountability all around you.

Actions

Do you still remember why you made the decision to no longer be a girlfriend but a wife? Just in case you need to refresh your mind, go back and rehearse the bait and what the trap creates. After assessing his answers, you will find yourself either intentionally no longer dating or intentionally one step closer to commitment.

Intentionally No Longer Dating

This may have been one of the toughest decisions you had to make, but the "exchange" is worth it. Allow God to love on you and heal your heart. Don't try to self-medicate yourself by quickly jumping into the face of another guy or turning to unhealthy habits to relieve the pain you may feel. Throw all of your emotional weight onto God. That means you are going to have to sit in it. Yes, sit in it! Sit in what you feel and think your way through this as you evaluate how you will approach dating the next go round, this time with a higher self-esteem, more confidence and a trust in God that you did not have before. Build yourself up in who you are by renewing your mind with truth. Here are a few books and practices that will help you do that.

Books

1. *The Holy Bible*

   Not an option. I suggest reading a chapter of the book of proverbs each day as a start

2. *Sex and the Single Girl,* by Dr. Juli Slattery
3. *25 Ways to Prepare for Marriage Other Than Dating,* by Jamal Miller
4. *The 5 Love Languages,* by Gary Chapman
5. *Sex and the Supremacy of Christ,* by John Piper and Justin Taylor

Practices

1. Read daily!

   Always have something of truth to meditate on to replace negative thoughts and to renew your mind. Knowledge fills our dark voids of the soul and understanding of that truth brings about contentment and satisfaction. You have to renew your mind to do that and reading is the fundamental start.

2. **Distance yourself** from places and people that will only cause you to go back or do something you know will be counteractive to your healing.

3. **Surround yourself** with wise counsel.

4. **Clean up your social media** to avoid triggers that will bring emotional stress.

5. If you don't have one already, **find a local community of believers or church home** to surround yourself with that will provide truth and accountability to move forward. A great counselor will help you as well.

6. **Remember and repeat this continually,** "What I am reaching for is greater than what I am leaving behind." This will strengthen you.

7. **Cry it out!** Crying relieves your mind and body of the hurt you feel and it helps flush things out. It took me a good 6 months after breaking up with my boyfriend to feel like I could live again and I cried my way through it. It's better to cry tears of healing that will help you swim instead tears of frustration and pain that will only drown you in the end.

8. **Be productive!!!!** Find things to do that take the focus off of you and put it on God and others. Find some girls to mentor, help someone who needs child care, find a place to volunteer, etc. Purpose (like what I'm doing now) has saved and continues to save me from settling and living an idle and convenient life. Queen, you have work to do. Let it fill your time.

Intentionally Dating (Courting)

If you are intentionally dating, that means you have removed yourself from him as a girlfriend and have made yourself available as a potential spouse, nothing more, nothing less. Refer to the writing exercise from Bait # 2, *Easy Access*, and the chapters *Your Way Of Escape* and *The Courting Relationship* to remember how to set boundaries. Here are a few steps that will help continue to push you towards commitment.

1. Set a maximum amount of time that you are willing to court. This will keep you guys from getting too relaxed and not progressing.

2. Get accountability IMMEDIATELY! I repeat this 100 times because it is so important!!! You are going to need all the help and wise counsel you can get to help you guys sort through difficult topics and past baggage that you didn't deal with before.

3. Learn about marriage! Become a student of God's heart and intentions behind marriage. A healthy start is Genesis ch. 1-3, Ephesians ch. 5, 1 Corinthians ch. 6-7, and 13 and 1, 2 and 3 John in the Bible. These are all chapters that I referenced earlier, as well as ALL the book references that I have listed so far. Take a moment to jot them all down and put them on your "to buy" list.

4. Sign up for marriage counseling! As you continue to learn more about each other, and there is no info that has caused you to count him out as a potential spouse, move towards counseling and setting a date to marry.

5. Still...be productive!

> "Find things to do that take the focus off of you and put it on others. Find some girls to mentor, help someone who needs child care, find a place to volunteer, etc. Purpose (like what I'm doing now) has saved and continues to save me from settling and living an idle and convenient life. Queen, you have work to do. Let it fill your time, whether you are single or married."

6. If at any time you find out that he is not someone that you can entrust your life to in marriage, go back to Intentionally Not Dating and begin a new journey of discovery.

Although I have given you steps that will help you move toward commitment, it's ultimately up to God to guide you through this process. Open yourself up to His leading and trust His sovereignty. He knows everything you don't and He won't lead you astray. Whether you are intentionally dating or not, you are a wife; to Christ first and always (a relationship with Him is marriage) and to a man second and optionally. You can't be a girlfriend and a wife at the same time and if you are practicing being a girlfriend then you are not preparing to be a wife.

> **#TheGirlfriendTrap**
>
> *If you are practicing being a girlfriend then you are not preparing to be a wife.*
>
> #TheGirlfriendTrap

I hope you have been encouraged to keep growing because I believe your life is packed with so much purpose. Be excited today and hopeful about tomorrow. With God, your life is only going to get better from here.

Next Steps

Are you on social media? Stay connected and let's continue the conversation where you will find me having more discussions about dating, sex, relationships and other good things in between. Let's make this a two-way conversation.

- Visit my website **www.SheAbundantly.com**

- Leave an AMAZING review on Amazon (QR codes on page 205)

- Subscribe to my YouTube Channel: **She Abundantly**

- Engage with me on **Instagram, tiktok** or **fb: @SheAbundantly**

- Text me your girlfriend stories/confessions at **708-580-8823**

- SHARE THIS BOOK with others! Take a picture of you and the book and post it with the hashtags **#TheGirlfriendTrap #SheAbundantly**. Don't forget to tag me in it. Let other ladies know how great this convo has been.

I hope to hear from you soon.

P.S. Don't forget to read the *Questions and Rebuttals* and *The Conversation with a Woman Who Was a Girlfriend for 10 Years* on the next few pages. Trust me, your heart will be glad you did.

CHAPTER 17
Questions and Rebuttals

You may have some questions and rebuttals that you are wrestling with after reading this. Let's see if I can help you with those.

1. Do I break up with my boyfriend?

You can't be a girlfriend and a wife at the same time. Not being a girlfriend is telling him that you are a wife. Let your worth be made known and how will it be if you continue to accept a relationship status that is beneath your worth? Remember the bait, what the trap creates and why it's necessary that you escape.

2. What if he walks away after I express my desire for commitment or tell him I no longer want to be a girlfriend?

He just showed you how much he values you and he doesn't believe you are worth him committing to. This is a blessing, meaning God is giving you an open door to advance, grow and go forward because you have been stuck in this relationship! Your standards just eliminated a guy who was not willing to value your time, heart and future. He is making room for the one who will.

P.S. You are the prize. Don't fret! He's just not the winner.

3. But I've only had one boyfriend.

Great! Let him be the first and the last. Just because you've only had one doesn't guarantee forever. It's still not commitment whether he's the 1st, 3rd or 10th guy. There is no greater time than now to set your price.

4. Verbal agreements hold up in court.

Not when it comes to marriage. A girlfriend has no rights in court or heaven.

5. If there is no title or if I don't claim him as mine, then he will play me and talk to other girls.

Only a guy who is not intentional about pursuing you will do that. That's a clear sign that he is not that into you or concerned about your heart and if that's the case, meet him with the same kind of energy. Never give a guy more than he is giving you. Even if you do become his girlfriend, if it's in his heart, he will still play you and string you along. He is not ready for commitment and is not on your level. Kindly show him to the door.

6. My momma / "whoever" was a girlfriend and she got married.

I have 3 objections to this way of thinking:

o She is not the standard, the truth is! The reason why people have made it to the other side is because of grace and mercy, not necessarily wisdom! She still took a huge chance on losing her investments. Think of it like this: 10 people jump into a den with one lion. The lion can only focus on one at a time to eat. This gives the other 9 people a chance to escape. They may have made it out alive, but it was not a wise decision to jump into the den in the first place.

o Did she make it to marriage with her physical, emotional and spiritual integrity? Most do not, and I mean most, which is very sad because it shows our lack of respect for God and self. It's also a challenge to enter into marriage with that kind of baggage as many never heal, allowing their past to cause divorce! This is more about integrity and honoring God than it is a ring. One time of sexual sin is just as damaging and detrimental as multiple and true love honors and protects, not takes for selfish pleasures.

"But among you there must not be even be a hint of sexual immorality, or of any kind of impurity, or of greed, because these are improper for God's holy people" – **Ephesians 5:3 (NIV)**

o   Are you willing to go through what she went through to get to marriage? If you could see the wounds that hide deep within her soul, you would think twice about taking the steps she took. Ponder on that one for a moment.

7. Life is one big risk and you only live once.

True…kind of! But not all risks are worth taking. Wisdom will tell you to make choices with the least amount of risk and you have a better chance of getting a bigger return in commitment than in any relationship outside of it. Your children are depending on you to make good decisions now. The consequences of your actions is what you will feed them.

8. Is it possible to be a girlfriend and still keep your integrity intact?

Yes and no! Yes, you can avoid sexual sin but it's very rare and this still gives a false sense of ownership along with all the other trappings. And simply put, when you enter into a system, you are saying yes to the end product that the system produces. All machinery will be in full motion, but that motion will be against you and not for you. Being his girlfriend works against teaching him your value and setting your price. The more you tell the brain, "my, my…mine" the more you get comfortable and boundaries begin to relax. It's not so much the title as it is the function. Courting sets mental boundaries and when you are constantly being reminded that he is not yours, and vice versa, it keeps you alert and careful to respect this situation as much as possible.

Plus, you want to create a standard, not just for you but for those around you and those coming up after you, especially your kids or future kids. My goal is to make the things of God known, not low self-esteem or a fear of missing out. I welcome you to follow me as I follow Christ.

9. A little intimate touch won't hurt anyone.

Certain intimate touches change things, telling the body to want each other before the brain and discernment can catch up. That, queen, is a form of manipulation as it controls or turns his choice towards you without thinking. Examples: rubbing, kissing, certain bodily embraces.

P.S. I encourage you to let the first touch be an explosive touch, one that commitment will allow total and complete freedom to play ;)

10. Isn't courting the same as being boyfriend and girlfriend? If not, should I court multiple people at once?

I say no to both questions and here's why I say that. There is a difference between exclusivity (boyfriend and girlfriend) and intentionality (courting) and I don't want us to confuse the two.

Exclusivity

Exclusive means to exclude every other person as a potential life partner. Boyfriends and girlfriends do this in a false way. They think they are exclusive but they are lying to themselves. It is a form of false commitment.

Courting someone does not mean that they are yours to have exclusively. It simply means you have decided to be intentional about getting to know this person with marriage in mind. They are free to walk away from the table at any moment and so are you, with no ownership or strings ever existing because it's still not commitment. An acceptance of a proposal from him is the sign that means you both are moving toward exclusivity. Once married, you both are officially exclusive, counting out all other possibilities for a spouse.

Intentionality

Courting multiple people at once is the cultural standard, but not a wise one in my opinion and here is why I say this. How can you truly give yourself to something if you are not fully present? It's like trying to watch multiple shows at once. In order to take anything in, you are going to have to ignore one show to listen to the other but both shows are happening at the same time (courting multiple people at the same time). With divided attention you can't reach optimal success.

I have never been successful at having divided attention (like studying for a test and talking to a friend at the same time) because I miss things. It causes delay and it causes me to back track, etc. How about you? In order to make a huge life decision like determining who you will bond with for a lifetime, you will need undivided attention and a clear mind. This approach is not claiming them as yours but it's being intentional with your goal to determine if they are for you to marry.

Court means to date "you" with the intention to marry... "you" (one person), not to marry... you and you and you. (multiple people).

Courting, in itself, is intentional and intentional means to aim at one target. By the time you get to courting, you have already seen something in that person that you want to focus on more. So courting multiple people defeats the concept of courting. If there are multiple people that one finds interesting, at some point you will have to narrow it down to one and focus on that one.

Think of this whole dating process like this:

- **Possible interest:** People are all in one room having a talk with everyone. (no commitment)
- **Courting**: Two people go to the side to have a one-on-one talk while still being in the room amongst others. (no commitment)
- **Marriage:** You two go off into a room by yourselves. (commitment)

CHAPTER 18

The Conversation with a Woman Who Was a Girlfriend for 10 Years

Meet Tiana Rogers, a 35-year-old woman who was a girlfriend for 10 years on and off with the same guy. She is now married to a new guy, 4 years now, and they dated 9 months before getting engaged.

Me: If you could do things differently when it came to dating, what would you change?

Tiana: Not looking to culture to inform me on how to date. I would tell my younger self to look to God, Christ, mentors and marriages that I admire to help me be intentional with dating. Dating is supposed to be with the intent to marry. I have heard so many people say, " we don't like titles," but I feel you are cheapening the value God has placed on you when you give husband privileges to a prospect.

Me: Why did you stay a girlfriend for so long?

Tiana: I stayed a girlfriend because I didn't know the practical steps on how to make a decision to not be one. I realize now that my then boyfriend wasn't sure about himself either. I stayed because I had invested so much time in the relationship. He'd known me since I was a teen and the history we had meant so much to me. Ultimately, my decision to stay was rooted in fear. At the time, I thought that he was the best God had for me. I didn't know that I didn't have to sacrifice parts of myself to be chosen, and that the greatest love is FREE!

Me: Why did you break up with your boyfriend for good?

Tiana: Through prayer and accountability groups through church, I made a decision to put my request out there to be married. I knew that he had a choice to respond to it or not. If he chose not to commit to me, I had grown in God enough to know that it wasn't a reflection of my value. Once I detached from the result of his decision, I became free from fear of losing the relationship. It wasn't easy but once I exchanged a man that I could see for the one that I couldn't, my entire life changed.

Me: What was his decision and what action did he take to show it?

Tiana: He chose not to commit and it showed by his lack of care. I got into a pretty severe car wreck around the same time that the relationship was fizzling out. When the accident happened, everyone showed up for me except him. He lived in another state at the time and waited over a month to come see me. He didn't show up in the way that mattered most to me. What I needed was a partner that was willing to drop everything and come to my aid. He had excuse after excuse. His actions showed me that I was not the #1 priority. I then had to decide if that was good enough for me. After he finally came to visit me, I knew that was the end. A few months later, I packed all his stuff with no notice and mailed it to him.

I chose not to talk to him because I knew if I did, he would talk me out of walking away from him for good. At his request, we met face to face about 6 months later and he asked me if I thought we should try our relationship one more time. It was painful but I chose not to listen to my heart or feelings. Instead, I listened to my spirit, my gut! I had to be willing to be open to the possibility that there was more for me!

I have learned that anything that you love more than God, the enemy will use it to break your heart. So, while I had a broken heart, I had a fixed vision for myself and the future.

Me: What were you hoping would happen in that relationship? Did you want more from the relationship?

Tiana: I was hoping that he would ask me to marry him. Every girl waits to be chosen; for a man to say "you are a wife." Years later, my ex did tell me that he knew I was always *a* wife from the day he met me. It took me some time to recognize that he was right, I just wasn't *his* wife.

Me: How did you heal from that breakup?

Tiana: I spent more time with myself and with the people I loved and that I knew loved me. I took my first trip alone. I decided that I wasn't going to wait for someone else to choose me. I chose myself. I made a list in advance of my standards so that when the next person came I wouldn't settle. My mentor and pastor challenged me to stop dating for a 'type' and start dating for a purpose.

Me: What would you say to women right now who are stuck in these dead end relationships.

Tiana: There is nothing you have to do to convince a man that you are the prize. Know that if a man does not have plans for you, then he's not your man. If he has doubts about committing to you, then you get to move on and that's okay. He will find someone better for him, and so will you. You don't have to beg or convince anyone to choose you. All you have to do is show up in your divine power. Women are designed to attract; we were never designed to chase. Your femininity is your superpower. When your heart is aligned with God's heart it allows you to show up in your full power. This position puts you in a place where you are not threatened by other women who show up in the same way or men who don't recognize it.

Dr. Tiana N Rogers – CEO of Mended Hope, a premium consulting company specializing in providing evidence-based strategies and frameworks to help high-impact women increase their resilience, influence, and impact through its Thrive Academy for Personal & Professional Development. You can learn more about Dr. Tiana and her work at www.mendedhope.org.

Appendix A: A Diagram of the Girlfriend Trap

The Girlfriend Trap

Illegal sex, hurt, rejection, Idolatry, dishonor, distrust, deceit, uncovered, broken family, generational curse, etc.

Easy Access
Bait

Sense of Self-worth
Bait

Exclusivity
Bait

The Boyfriend
FAKE Covering

Low self-esteem

Lacking Connection

Lacking Commitment

The Girlfriend
Lacking Covering

Draw a line from each deficiency that the girl has to the bait that she would be attracted to

Leave a positive review for this book on **Amazon**

Visit my **Website**

Subscribe to my **YouTube Channel**

References

Abma, Joyce C and Gladys M. Martinez. "Sexual Activity and Contraceptive Use Among Teenagers in the United States, 2011–2015." *CDC/National Center for Health Statistics*, 22 June 2017, www.cdc.gov/nchs/pressroom/nchs_press_releases/2017/201706_N SFG.htm

Britannica, The Editors of Encyclopaedia. "adenosine triphosphate." *Encyclopedia Britannica*, 12 March 2020, www.britannica.com/science/adenosine-triphosphate

Contributors, New World Encyclopedia. "Concubinage." *New World Encyclopedia,* 17 March 2017, www.newworldencyclopedia.org/p/index.php?title=Concubinage&old id=1003774

Getlen, Larry. "The Fascinating History of How Courtship Became Dating." *New York Post*, 15 March 2016, www.nypost.com/2016/05/15/the-fascinating-history-of-how-courtship-became-dating/

Hotline, National Domestic Violence. "Domestic Violence Statistics." *The Hotline*, www.thehotline.org/stakeholders/domestic-violence-statistics/

Kramer, Stephanie. "U.S. Has World's Highest Rate of Children Living in Single-Parent Households." *Pew Research Center,* 19 Dec. 2019 www.pewrsr.ch/2LLvbxW

Markarlan, Taylor. "How Dating Has Changed Over The Last 100 Years." *The List,* 3 May 2017, *UPDATED: 22 AUG 2019,* www.thelist.com/62575/dating-changed-last-100-years/?utm_campaign=clip

Piper, John and Justin Taylor. *Sex and the Supremacy of Christ*, Crossway, 2005.

Smith, *Christopher R.* "What is the Difference Between Wives and Concubines?" *Good Question Blog, 12* June 2021, www.google.com/amp/s/goodquestionblog.com/2021/06/12/what-is-the-difference-between-wives-and-concubines/amp/

"The Decline of Marriage and Rise of New Families." *Pew Research Center,* 18 Nov. 2010, www.pewresearch.org/social-trends/2010/11/18/ii-overview/

"U.S. Abortion Statistics." *Abort73.com,* 2 Jan. 2022, www.abort73.com/abortion_facts/us_abortion_statistics/

Made in the USA
Columbia, SC
08 June 2023